The Thirties

An illustrated
History in colour
1930-1939

By
R J Unstead

A PLEASANT TRIP TO
GERMANY

Macdonald Educational

Introduction
The Thirties

Contents

A MACDONALD BOOK

© Macdonald Educational Ltd 1974

First published in Great Britain in 1974
Reprinted 1974, 1982, 1985

ISBN 0 356 04093 3

Printed and bound in Great Britain by
Purnell and Sons (Book Production) Ltd
Paulton, Bristol

Published by
Macdonald & Company (Publishers) Ltd
Maxwell House
74 Worship Street
London EC2A 2EN

Members of BPCC plc

The thirties was a bleak decade dominated by fear. It began with the Depression which spread round the world bringing unemployment to millions of workers and fostering the social conditions in which Hitler and some lesser dictators came to power.

Fear of Communism played its part in establishing the dictators, and terrorism became a potent weapon to subdue civilian populations. The Western democracies were so obsessed by fear of war that they became incapable of averting the disaster which they dreaded.

But there was a brighter side to the thirties. The New Deal in America revived hope that man could manage his own affairs more justly. Away from distressed areas, many people enjoyed a better standard of life and an almost dazzling choice of entertainment. Notable advances took place in science, medicine, industry and transport. This was an era that laid down the shape of our lives today.

◁ **German poster for Hitler Youth.**

▷ **Despair in the thirties:** an American migrant leaves his dust-destroyed farm.

Shock Waves of the Crash

The collapse of the New York Stock Market in October 1929 proved to be a turning point in history; it led to a catastrophic depression that spread all over the world.

△ **Brazilian revolutionaries** in 1930 when half the public employees were out of work and exports dropped by 40 per cent.

People suddenly had less money to spend and invest, or, if they had money, they had lost the confidence and even the will to put things right. Business faltered; men and women were thrown out of work. Since people could now buy less, more factories closed.

In Europe, countries which had relied on American loans were asked to repay them. Austria's biggest bank closed down and, in Germany, six million workers lost their jobs. Britain's depressed industries, which had been in the doldrums throughout the twenties, became even more depressed. Her traditional industries—coal, steel, textiles, shipbuilding—suffered worst.

For a time, the French franc stayed firm, but France (unlike Russia) was part of the world's economic system and bound to suffer like the rest.

The Depression spread like an epidemic. American loans had supported the economy of Latin America and Eastern Europe, where prices of products like coffee and wheat dropped disastrously. Cuba's sugar exports fell to a quarter of their 1924 value; Poland's trade declined to less than a third of its 1929 level; Brazilian and Japanese exports fell by over 30 per cent, Australia's and Canada's by over 25 per cent.

In a world where millions of people went hungry, farmers burnt their crops and refused to plant seed. Food prices had fallen too low to make farming worthwhile.

△ **Unemployed!** The man has no job, his wife next to no money. Some countries, like Britain and Germany, provided money for the unemployed, just enough for bare necessities; in others, like the United States and France, the unemployed had to rely on local relief.

▷ **Germany:** a camp for the unemployed made from junk. One out of two Germans between 16 and 30 was without work, a desperate situation which the Nazis were able to exploit, cunningly uniting all who looked for a way out of Germany's distress.

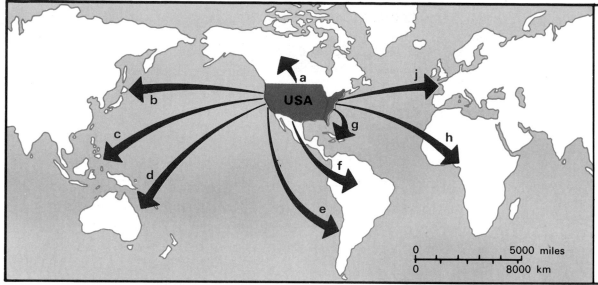

How the depression affected the rest of the world

a Grain prices fall
b Silk and Cotton prices fall
c Tin and Rubber prices fall
d Wool prices fall
e Meat prices fall
f Coffee prices fall
g Sugar prices fall
h Cocoa prices fall
j Europe's industry collapses

0   5000 miles
0   8000 km

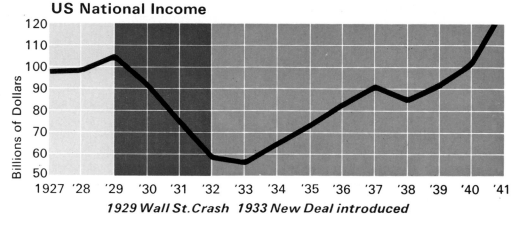

US National Income

Billions of Dollars

120
110
100
90
80
70
60
50

1927 '28 '29 '30 '31 '32 '33 '34 '35 '36 '37 '38 '39 '40 '41

1929 Wall St. Crash   1933 New Deal introduced

◁ **Table** showing how the U.S. economy fluctuated during the thirties. Recovery took several years and there was a setback in 1937. Unemployment remained staggeringly high until rearmament brought increasing prosperity in the forties.

▽ **Austrians** searching through refuse in the market place in hope of finding something to eat. Yet wheat was rotting in the fields, unsaleable. Austria, reduced by the Treaty of Versailles to one eighth of its former size, had been in a precarious position and specially dependent upon American loans. When these were recalled, the economy collapsed.

Life in the Depression

People who lived through the Depression have never forgotten the anguish of those times, the stark contrast between rich and poor, the absurdity of food being destroyed and the helplessness of man to order his own affairs.

△ **Dancing to Roy Fox and his band** in London. South-east England suffered much less from the Depression than the old industrial areas. Those who had jobs could enjoy an evening out for remarkably little, since prices remained low.

The saddest feature of the Depression was the queue of unemployed workers. There were 12 to 15 million out of work in the United States, six million in Germany until Hitler came to power, nearly three million in Britain, and countless others throughout the world. Being out of work brought hurt to a man's pride and actual want to his family.

When the Depression came, America had no national system of unemployment benefit; each state provided its own measures, such as money payments, relief work and free soup. In some states, relief was practically non-existent.

Thousands took to the road, looking for work, begging and thieving and living in squalid camps by rail tracks. Farm prices fell so low that corn was used to heat court-houses because it was cheaper than coal. And in those court-houses, farmers heard the judge put them off their land because they could not meet bank loans. Milk was poured away and animals were killed and burned in hope of better prices. The Negroes' plight was desperate in both the cotton-growing South and the industrial north, where the Negro was "last hired, first fired".

In Britain, an unemployed man with wife and children received about £1.50, just enough at that time to feed them at a low level. With no margin for clothes, household goods or pleasure, perhaps a quarter of the nation was ill-nourished, ill-clad and badly housed.

Revolutions and riots occurred in some countries and, as capitalism seemed to have failed, many turned to Fascism or Communism. Yet, generally speaking, the poor were amazingly docile, even apathetic. In the Western world, apart from in Mussolini's Italy and Hitler's Germany, the birth rate fell, as though parents dreaded bringing children into such a world.

On the other hand, those with jobs and money found life enjoyable. Food, clothes, houses and motoring were cheap. In areas with new industries, such as light engineering and radio, chemicals and car manufacture, workers enjoyed a good standard of living. It was in the old industrial areas and in farming communities that people really suffered.

◁ **A French working-class family at home** in the thirties. France, less dependent upon industry and exports than Britain and Germany, seemed in a better position. By 1932-33, however, the slump in world trade had brought hunger and even starvation to many workers.

△ **Jarrow marchers** lining up for corned beef and potatoes at a farm near Bedford in 1936. Jarrow, a ship-building town in north-east England, had nearly 80 per cent of its workers unemployed and to draw attention to their plight, 200 men marched to London. This helped towards the founding of new industries.

▽ **1931 General Election poster** in Britain. It shows the plight of mothers and children against the background of unemployment.

△ **Children at play** in a slum tenement in America where poverty and unemployment induced many to take to crime as a means of surviving.

Fashion

Dress generally became brighter and more varied; there were several styles of fashion at any one time, so people were freer to choose what they wanted to wear.

△ **Wives of unemployed** set out on a demonstration march, 1933. Their clothes, shabby and unfashionable, probably came from a second-hand dealer or were home-made.

As the thirties progressed, women's dress became more feminine. They gave up the boyish look of the twenties and had their hair permanently waved, often in the style of Hollywood film stars. They put on make-up, nail varnish, bangles, earrings and necklaces.

Every smart woman wore an entrancing hat and, at fashionable weddings and garden parties, a light fragile dress to the ankles. Squared shoulders came in, with the well-tailored look and two-piece cardigan suits. Backless evening gowns revealed the feminine shape and, from the knee, broke out into flounces.

Practical inventions influenced fashions. Clothes became easier to get into, as zip-fasteners arrived and elastic and press-studs replaced tapes and hooks-and-eyes. Men's wear was becoming slightly less formal, as the younger ones took to wearing coloured shirts with their sports jackets, grey flannels and suede shoes. Even their underwear changed when cellular-weave vests and elastic-topped shorts replaced the old heavy woollen undergarments.

△ **1938 advertisement for cami-knickers of printed crepe with rayon.** Rayon came into use in the twenties, nylon in the thirties.

△ **Seeing passengers off** on the *Coronation Scot,* 1937. The well-dressed man wears a long, belted, double-breasted overcoat, with patch pockets, wide revers and turned-back cuffs, wide trousers with turn-ups, a soft-brimmed trilby hat and wash-leather gloves. The girls wear tailored suits and sling-back shoes.

◁ **In a London milk-bar,** about 1936. The fashion-conscious Duchess of Kent had introduced eye-veils on hats, some of fine mesh, others of coarse fish-net. Her innumerable hats, freely copied, include this Breton sailor type, immense picture hats, a jaunty little pork-pie hat, a man's Homburg and a pierrot-like cap. George V's death in 1936 brought black into fashion for a time, but colours returned with the Coronation of 1937, especially powder-blue, the Queen's favourite shade. 1938 saw a return of Edwardian coiffures, evening dresses and wide-brimmed hats, but there was no single fashion; women now wore what they liked or what suited them.

△ **In the mid-thirties, emphasis fell upon the shoulders.** Leg-of-mutton sleeves, small waists, capes, ruffles and frills on dresses all helped to give the wide-shouldered look. Hat styles included masculine types like the little bowler and the trilby with its brim tilted down over one eye.

△ **Sportswear in the thirties:** notice the eye-shades, ankle-socks and cravats. Some of these styles, like the divided skirt and the long plus-fours, never caught on, but shorts had come to stay. The sun-bathing habit and cheap holiday cruises had a brightening effect on leisure wear.

Art Deco

Art Deco (the name comes from the exhibition of Arts Decoratifs, Industriels et Modernes in Paris, 1925) is the term used to describe a decorative style of the twenties and thirties. It affected architecture, clothes and domestic interiors.

The style grew out of the Art Nouveau movement in the early years of the century. Artists had shown that even in an industrial age, design could be both colourful and imaginative. The later arrival of Diaghilev's Russian Ballet in Paris caused great excitement with its exotic costumes and colours, orange, violet and vivid green.

Then came the emergence of Cubism and Negro art, to be followed in the twenties by the emphasis which Bauhaus artists placed on clean lines and geometric shapes. Alongside these influences, there existed a liking for lively, jazzy decorations, expressing the vivacity of the times, and a taste for the arresting designs of Ancient Egypt and Aztec Mexico.

Art Deco took over the Bauhaus aim to form a union between art and industry. It adjusted design to meet industry's needs and encouraged artists to come to terms with machine production. New methods and materials in mass production assisted the aims of the style. Art Deco entered into the design of almost everything, from Corbusier's buildings, hotel foyers, and lounges of luxury liners to wireless-sets and table-lamps.

At its best, the style had a dynamic vigour, a clarity and a joyous simplicity; at its worst, it became the victim of mass production, vulgar, trivial and ornate. Though essentially a style of the inter-war years, Art Deco still survives in Pop Art.

△ **French company advertisement,** which includes a typical example of Art Deco lettering; this has become a permanent feature of modern poster design.

▽ **Belgian tobacco jar of the thirties,** which has a Cubist flavour in the design and also echoes the shape of an Aztec temple. The result is preposterous.

▽ **Suburban garden gate** with rising sun design, a popular Art Deco symbol, frequently seen on wireless cabinets and household objects.

▷ **Interior of the Granada cinema,** Tooting, London, in which Gothic and Moorish architectural styles are combined to produce an exotic environment.

Art Deco was also to be seen in hotel foyers like that of the Strand Palace Hotel, London, in Cunard and Orient liners and in some big stores. Its lavish ornamentation and strident colours (though there was also a taste for muted shades of pink and grey) contrasted strangely with the functional simplicity of Bauhaus design. Compared with Corbusier's buildings, the later extravagances of Art Deco appear pretentious and absurdly ornate.

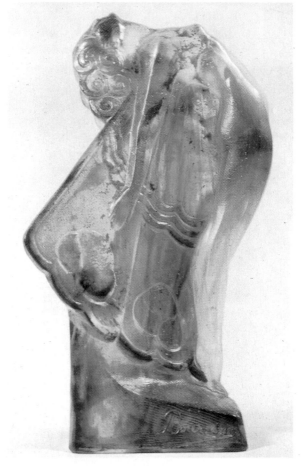

◁ **Figure of green translucent glass,** typical of the thirties. Dogs straining at the leash, girls with streaming hair and female figures with diaphanous draperies were other favourites. They appeared as ornaments, table lamp bases and on decorative panels and motor car bonnets.

△ **French cigarette case,** stream-lined in shape, with zig-zag lightning flash. This device could be seen in the Nazi S.S. badge and was meant to be a dynamic symbol, proclaiming youth and virility.

The Nazis Take Over

Hitler emerged as German Chancellor in January 1933, not as the result of a revolutionary coup, but apparently in accordance with the constitution.

Since 1918, Germany had suffered the humiliation of defeat, attempts at revolution, occupation of the Ruhr and disastrous inflation. The German people had had little experience of democracy. The Republic, set up in 1919, was never liked by the Nationalists on the Right or the Communists on the Left.

In the *Reichstag* (parliament), parties split into squabbling groups and the public became wearily used to feeble cabinets and semi-dictatorial rule by the President. But although the government was unpopular, most Germans still respected authority. Hitler realized that he must come to power by apparently legal means.

In 1928, the Nazis had only twelve seats in the Reichstag but, by 1930, they had won 107 seats. As the Depression hit Germany, more and more people listened to Hitler who laid the blame for the troubles upon the Jews, Communists and the Treaty of Versailles.

The elections of 1932 gave the Nazis 230 seats, but this was not a parliamentary majority. However, to confound the Communist Party which had polled four and a half million votes, von Papen, leader of the Catholic Centre Party, proposed an alliance with the Nazis. Hitler would be Chancellor, von Papen vice-Chancellor. Privately, von Papen and President Hindenburg thought they could use Hitler as a puppet; they, the army and the powerful industrialists would keep him in order. Hitler had other ideas.

As soon as he became Chancellor, he demanded power to govern by emergency decrees (permitted in exceptional circumstances by the constitution). The Reichstag building was burnt down, the country was kept in a ferment and, with Nazi Storm Troopers arresting their opponents, Hitler obtained the two-thirds majority needed to change the constitution. Thus, he gained the power to draft laws without parliamentary consent. The Republic was closed down overnight. Hitler became ruler of Germany.

△ **Jackbooted Storm Trooper** displays a Nazi leaflet during the election of March 1933. The Nazis won 288 seats, a bare majority, but the arrest of Communist deputies and the support of the Catholic Centre gave Hitler the two-thirds majority he needed to change the constitution. The Social Democrats were the only party with the courage to oppose him, but the Bill to free the government from parliamentary control was passed by 441 votes to 94.

△ **Nazi troopers and students** about to burn "degenerate" books and magazines. Any work which conflicted with the Nazi philosophy was banned and Goebbels instituted strict censorship. Many writers disappeared or fled abroad.

△ **President Hindenburg and the new Chancellor, Adolf Hitler,** in Berlin. The old man's prestige was useful. When he died in 1934, Hitler assumed absolute power.

△ **The Reichstag on fire,** February 1933. The Nazis announced that the parliament building had been set alight by a young Dutchman, van der Lubbe, acting on Communist orders. Others believed that the S.A. had deliberately started the fire to provoke public alarm. Whatever the truth, the fire gave Hitler the excuse to suspend the constitution's guarantee of individual liberty. The Nazis intensified their measures against their opponents.

△ **S.S. dagger** inscribed *My Honour is Loyalty* and **S.A. dagger** inscribed *All for Germany*. The S.A. were Storm Troopers recruited from early days for street-fighting and battering opponents, an unruly force which Hitler liquidated in 1934. The S.S. was an élite body of fanatical Nazis, disciplined and devoted to the *Führer*.

◁ **Arrested Communists** guarded by an S.A. member. The Communists had also worked for the German Republic's downfall, thinking that the Nazis would soon collapse and leave the way open for revolution. But Hitler speedily crushed them.

13

Hitler's Germany

△ **German poster showing a member of the Hitler Youth,** with the *Führer* behind him. All children over six had to join the Hitler Youth; they were taught the Nazi faith and, when older, they served in labour battalions; girls did household or farm service.

△ **"Butcher of Berlin",** a French comment on the Night of the Long Knives, 1934, when Hitler ordered the massacre of thousands of S.A. members. The S.A., so useful for battering opponents, had become an embarrassment when it got out of hand.

▷ **Nazi rally, Nuremburg 1934.** Enormous rallies were a feature of the régime; they kept enthusiasm at fever-pitch and provided set pieces for Hitler's speeches.

Hitler had promised the rebirth of Germany. He would provide jobs, get rid of the Jews, tear up the Treaty of Versailles.

Through incessant propaganda, the people were made to feel that Germany was reborn. A master race of blond Nordic heroes had emerged, it was claimed, and no traitors must be allowed to interfere with their triumphant march. Trade unions and all political parties, except the Nazis, were closed down. No Jew was allowed to hold an official post; Jewish businesses were wrecked and thousands of Jews fled, or were sent to concentration camps.

To win the minds of the young, teachers were told what to teach, and the universities were made to put over theories of racial superiority. A man's duty was to fight, a woman's to bear children for the Fatherland. House-wives were even exhorted to give their gold rings to help the country's finances.

Hitler had to solve one problem. The S.A.'s violence disgusted generals and industrialists whose support was essential. Moreover, some S.A. leaders wanted to take over the Army and to institute an all-out revolution. So, on 30 June 1934, hundreds of S.A. members were massacred.

A campaign called *Battle for Work* reduced unemployment through public works and rearmament. For millions of Germans, Nazism meant a job and a feeling of national pride. In 1935, Germany regained the Saar (an area on the French frontier previously administered by the League of Nations) and Hitler defied the Treaty of Versailles by introducing conscription. A year later, he reoccupied the Rhineland. Germany was a Great Power again and 98.8 per cent of the people voted their approval of Hitler's policy.

◁ **Map of Germany,** showing the Rhineland (shaded area), which, by the Treaty of Versailles, was to be a permanently demilitarized zone. Having earlier announced conscription and the formation of a German army, Hitler sent troops into the Rhineland on 7 March 1936. The German General Staff was appalled by the risk but Hitler correctly guessed that France and Britain would not take up arms.

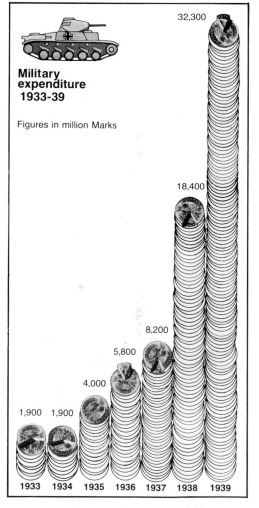

Military expenditure 1933-39

Figures in million Marks

32,300

18,400

8,200

5,800

4,000

1,900 1,900

1933 1934 1935 1936 1937 1938 1939

△ **Diagram showing Germany's increasing expenditure on arms.** This placed a terrific strain on the economy; people had to go short of domestic goods (*Guns before butter* was the slogan) and a programme was launched to produce synthetic food.

◁ **Poster of 1938,** showing a *Volkswagen,* the *People's Car,* and the coin that would pay for it. Hitler himself is said to have thought up the scheme whereby German workers would save five marks a week towards the purchase of a car. Millions of marks were paid over but no one received a car, because war broke out in September 1939.

Sport

Sport, increasingly run for profit on professional lines, played a big part in people's lives. Most were spectators, though more youngsters were now getting the chance to play games.

△ **Fred Perry,** Britain's best ever tennis player became the first player to win the "grand slam", the world's four major single titles in one year—Wimbledon, the U.S., French and Australian championships.

The older sports, such as football, cricket, horse racing and American baseball, attracted bigger followings than ever, and newer sports like speedway racing, wrestling, snooker and greyhound racing also drew crowds.

Britain, traditionally the founder country of many sports, could no longer claim supremacy in any field, except perhaps in soccer. Arsenal F.C. was the outstanding club of the thirties, and continental and Latin American sides were not yet a power in the game. The visit of a foreign team provided light relief compared with the stern encounters of the matches with Scotland, Ireland and Wales.

At golf, Bobby Jones and W. Hagen led the world, until Henry Cotton won the British Open in 1934 and 1937. Tennis honours were still shared between the United States, France and Australia, but Fred Perry of Britain was supreme for several years. The best women players were Helen Wills Moody, Alice Marble of the U.S. and Dorothy Round of Britain.

Britain's Sidney Wooderson broke long distance running records, but Jesse Owens, the American Negro, was the outstanding athlete of his time. Apart from Primo Carnera (Italy), Max Schmeling (Germany) and Kid Berg (Britain), the world's leading boxers were Americans. Joe Louis was perhaps the greatest heavyweight champion, while Henry Armstrong held three world championships in 1938.

Cricket was practically a private concern of the British Commonwealth, with the England-Australia Test matches outshining all others. Though England's W. Hammond and L. Hutton broke records, the feats of Don Bradman usually brought victory to the Australians until 1938. "Bodyline" bowling (where the bowler aims at the batsman rather than the wicket) was practised by the Englishman Larwood. In 1932–33, it almost produced a crisis in Commonwealth relations, but cricket managed to survive the rumpus.

△ **Poster of the German** *Strength through Joy* **movement.** Healthy outdoor activities like hiking and camping acquired great popularity. Youth hostels, founded in Germany in the twenties, sprang up in other countries.

△ **"Open Air Sports",** a satirical comment by the cartoonist Pont. Despite the popularity of outdoor activities, the thirties also saw a great increase in the number of "armchair sportsmen". Football Pools, which attracted enormous public support during this period, gave people a special interest in the sports results.

△ **Jesse Owens,** possibly the greatest sprinter who ever lived. In 1935, at Ann Arbor, Michigan, he broke six world records in 45 minutes—100 yards, long jump, 220 yards, 200 metres and the 220 yards and 200 metres low hurdles.

△ **German magazine** cover of the Berlin Olympics.

The Berlin Olympics

The 1936 Olympic Games were held in Berlin, where the Nazis put on a dazzling show to demonstrate to the world their efficiency and friendliness and also the supremacy of Nordic athletes. Alas for their hopes, the star of the Games proved to be Jesse Owens, an American Negro who won four gold medals. Negroes won several other golds and silvers, so upsetting Hitler that he left the arena, refusing to acknowledge their prowess. It was some consolation that the Germans won most gold medals overall, including the hammer, javelin and shot.

PLAYER'S CIGARETTES

D. G. BRADMAN (N. S. WALES)

△ **Don Bradman,** who dominated the England-Australia Tests in the thirties. In 1938, his average was 115·66 and in 80 Test innings, he made 29 centuries.

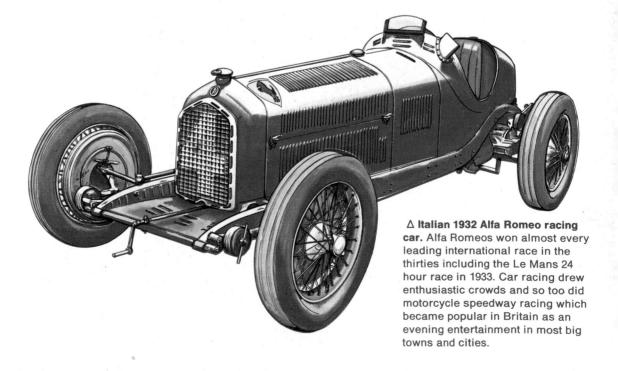

△ **Italian 1932 Alfa Romeo racing car.** Alfa Romeos won almost every leading international race in the thirties including the Le Mans 24 hour race in 1933. Car racing drew enthusiastic crowds and so too did motorcycle speedway racing which became popular in Britain as an evening entertainment in most big towns and cities.

American Society

Although the twenties had generally been a period of booming prosperity, the Depression had already begun in parts of the United States even before the crash of 1929.

The trouble with the American economy during this period was the uneven distribution of wealth. The rich were too rich and there were too few of them; the poor were too numerous and could afford to spend very little. If profits had been more evenly shared, if wages had been increased, if sick industries like coal-mining, textiles, the railroads and farming had been given help, this great country would have coped with a Stock Market crisis.

There were of course many Americas. There were the thriving industrial cities of the east. There was California, with its film-making, fruit and oil wells, Texas with its cattle and oil, the midwest, with its farming and manufactures, Florida, where the millionaires disported themselves.

There were also areas of poverty and backwardness—the south, where cotton farming was in a bad way and where wages and social conditions remained at their lowest. There were the farmlands of the west where the Great Plains suffered from drought and duststorms, the run-down quarters of great cities where poor immigrants and Negroes inhabited slums and ghettos.

Many Americans, from President Hoover down, believed sincerely in individualism. Profits and losses were the sole concern of individual businessmen. It was no part of the Government's business to fix prices or guarantee production costs. The tax system favoured the wealthy in the belief that they would use their money to start new industries and create more jobs.

When strikes occurred, these were generally short-lived, for the government favoured the employers against the workers. The unions were also hampered by small membership and by the "open shop" principle, whereby non-union workers had the same rights as unionists. In any case, the unions showed little interest in the unskilled worker or the Negro.

Corruption was a national disease. It was rife, not merely among police officers bribed by bootleggers (illegal traders in alcohol), but in the highest circles. In the twenties, officials close to the President were involved in scandals and, in the thirties, Huey Long, a popular champion of the poor, openly ruled the state of Louisiana by violence and bribery. Prohibition of alcohol came to an end in 1933, but it was harder to wipe out the corruption.

Thus, the country was in no condition to meet a crisis. When it came, panic was followed by near-collapse.

△ **Detail from a painting called** *The Soda Fountain* by William Glackens. The girl has a date with a young man and is waiting for him to arrive at the soda fountain in the corner of a drug store. Every town had its soda fountain which served as the meeting place for young people. At this time, young middle class Americans had far more money than most European youngsters; infinitely more of them attended High School and college. With their dating, joy-riding and parties, they established a tradition of teenage freedom.

▷ **1935 cartoon** gives the ordinary man's view of psychoanalysis: the doctor says "Keep telling yourself, 'I ain't nuts. I ain't nuts. I ain't nuts.'' This is a skit on the American obsession with psychoanalysis (study and treatment of the mind). Well-off men and women would regularly consult a psychoanalyst, confessing their inner thoughts, in hope of getting rid of tensions.

◁ **A farmer and his sons run for shelter** in a dust storm, Oklahoma, 1936. American farming, already hit by overproduction and low prices, suffered a series of disasters in the mid-thirties.

The southern Great Plains of Kansas, Oklahoma, Texas, New Mexico and Colorado had experienced drought. Then, in 1933, high winds swept the top soil from the fields, swamping crops, forming sand-dunes, obliterating roads and half-burying farmsteads.

The stricken region, known as the Dust Bowl, continued to suffer similar storms which ruined hundreds of farmers and caused widespread pneumonia. The country came to resemble a desert. But the farmers were largely to blame for soil erosion. They had ploughed up and over-cropped the grasslands, so there was nothing to prevent high winds from sweeping away the parched powdery soil.

△ **Negro children living in slum conditions.** Of all deprived Americans, the Negroes suffered worst during the Depression years.

▷ *American Gothic* by Grant Wood, a brilliant portrait of the narrow, pious, hard-working farmers who were the backbone of rural America.

The New Deal

△ **Stamp** commemorating the National Recovery Act of 1933, which greatly helped American farming.

▽ **Roosevelt** shakes hands with a miner during his Presidential campaign of 1932 when he defeated Herbert Hoover by an overwhelming margin. As almost always, Roosevelt is seen sitting down, for he had been crippled by polio and afterwards could neither stand nor walk unaided.

"I pledge myself to a new deal for the American people . . . the only thing we have to fear is fear itself."

Franklin D. Roosevelt, who opened his Presidency with these words, possessed idealism, fighting-spirit and drive. Above all, he convinced Americans that he cared about the ordinary man and would tackle the problems of poverty, injustice and unemployment.

As soon as he had taken office, he called Congress to a special session lasting one hundred days. During this time, with unprecedented speed, laws were passed to reform banking, to improve unemployment relief, to aid industry and farming and to end Prohibition. He set up agencies to rescue the country from the Depression. The schemes included a vast programme of public works, and the Tennessee Valley Authority to restore a huge area of farmland while generating cheap electrical power.

The rescue work succeeded. Unemployment came down by about five million; business, industry and farming began to recover. Sweeping measures for social security relieved some of the misery of the poor.

The New Deal was not an unqualified success. It had to face opposition from many who regarded Roosevelt as a wicked Socialist and it failed to abolish unemployment.

However, Roosevelt was the greatest American of modern times. He taught the people to look to the President to solve their troubles; he restored a good measure of the country's prosperity and gave the nation back its self-confidence.

△ **Work on an irrigation ditch in Arizona,** part of the programme to improve agriculture. Steps were taken to check soil erosion, to improve water supply and free tenant farmers from debt.

△ **Poster on a Californian highway,** produced for an advertising campaign to aid business and promote confidence in the recovery programme.

△ **Victim of the New Deal's shortcomings**— an unemployed youth in Washington. The government spent a lot but not enough, and there were still eight to nine million unemployed in 1939.

▷ **The Watts Bar Dam under construction** on the Tennessee River. Despite bitter opposition from private companies, Congress created the Tennessee Valley Authority in 1933 to harness the great Tennessee River and prevent the annual floods that devastated the area.

Serving seven States, TVA built 16 dams to bring agricultural prosperity and to provide electricity for industry and homes. Government funds were used by the PWA (Public Works Administration) to build dams in other parts of the country, such as Bonneville Dam on the Columbia River. Also built were airports, highways, tunnels, sewage systems, water supplies and workers' apartments.

Latin America in Turmoil

Until the Depression, Latin America was mostly ruled by dictators and the masses played little part in politics. The Crash produced a decade of violence but little social change.

▽ **Map of South America,** showing its political divisions. Brazil was the biggest country, but Argentina had a greater agricultural and industrial capacity. Until the Crash, beef was the major export, with coffee, (75% of the world's production) from Brazil; Chile produced nitrates and copper, Bolivia had rich tin mines, Venezuela produced oil, and Argentina was a major wheat and beef producing country. Foreign investment was mostly in mining, electrical power, transport and oil.

The continent had relied on export of raw materials and an abundance of foreign capital. When these were cut, the ruling classes, saddled with huge debts and empty treasuries, had to face the anger of the urban populations.

Revolutions, strikes and military coups became commonplace and drastic changes occurred as the poorer groups set up parties and searched for new leaders. A few were honest but most were rabble-rousers who used popular discontents to gain dictatorial power.

Peru's president, Leguia, was overthrown; Jose Uriburu became dictator of Argentina; Getulio Vargas survived civil war in Brazil. Alessandri was Chile's strong man until ousted by a Left-wing Popular Front. In Mexico, Cardenas introduced reforms that appealed to workers and peasants.

While most countries experienced violent upheavals at home, Bolivia and Paraguay fought the disastrous Chaco War (1932-35) in which each side lost a quarter of its fighting men.

By the late thirties, power had returned to the traditional classes, except in Chile and Mexico. The absence of social change in this period helps to explain Latin America's underdevelopment today. Nevertheless, in Mexico, Brazil, Colombia and Chile, industrial production almost doubled in ten years.

South America, 1930

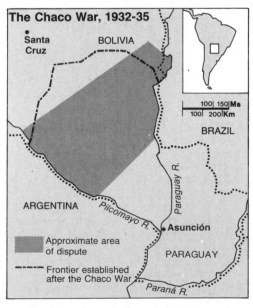

△ **Map showing the Chaco,** the area disputed by Bolivia and Paraguay.

▷ **Bolivian flag-bearer with his guard:** both sides were equipped with old-fashioned weapons. Paraguay, the poorer country, won the struggle with undercover help from Argentina.

Aviation

The thirties saw the establishment of commercial air routes throughout the world. International air races and continuous research improved aircraft performance.

Long distance flying was still a hazardous business in 1930. In that year, Amy Johnson flew solo from England to Australia in 19 days, narrowly failing to beat the record! However, nothing deterred the airlines and the pioneer pilots from developing commercial flying.

By 1932, a regular service had been started between London and Capetown; Colonel Lindbergh made a 29,000 mile air tour in 1933 to survey the world routes. England and Australia were linked by an airmail service in 1934, and, by island hopping, passengers could fly from San Francisco to Hong Kong in 1937.

Crossing the North Atlantic posed a particular problem because no aircraft could yet fly for 2,000 miles without re-fuelling. Various airlines made trial flights via the Azores and, in 1939, the Boeing 314 flying boat, *Yankee Clipper*, made the first airmail flight from New York to Spain and England.

Difficulties in setting up aerodromes had led to the production of long distance flying boats which could land in harbours, lakes and rivers. Britain's *Short Empire* was the first monoplane flying boat in service. Pan American Airways produced the *Glenn-Martin M130* and the *Sikorsky S-42*, both four-engined all-metal monoplanes.

Biplanes began to go out of fashion, as single wings were designed to give better air-lift than the old type. Light metal alloys took the place of fabric covering and, by 1939, Britain possessed two fast monoplane fighters in the *Hurricane* and *Spitfire*.

△ **Handover of mail bag** after the first Australia to England airmail service, 1934. Imperial Airways extended their service to Singapore in 1933. The link was completed when Qantas, the Australian company, carried mail from Singapore to Brisbane.

▷ *Handley-Page 42*, last and greatest of the biplane airliners.

◁ **Amy Johnson** who became a popular heroine. She flew solo to Australia in 1930.

△ **Wreckage of Britain's** *R101* **airship** when it crashed in France on its maiden flight in 1930. Airships had seemed to be the answer for long distance flying, for their size enabled them to carry ample fuel and to provide spacious accommodation for passengers. The German *Graf Zeppelin* made world flights and Britain built the *R100* and *R101* only to lose the latter in a disastrous crash.

Germany persisted and opened a trans-atlantic service with the *Hindenburg*; however, it burst into flames at its mooring in New York in 1937 (see page 54). A number of other accidents occurred, causing airships to be abandoned for passenger services.

△ **The** *Short-Mayo Composite* **aircraft of 1938**, consisting of the flying boat *Maia* which took off with the 4-engine seaplane, *Mercury*, on her back. The smaller aircraft could not take off with full fuel tanks but, at a safe height, she was released and flew from Ireland to Montreal with the first commercial cargo.

▽ *Supermarine S6B,* flown by Flight Lieut. Boothman at an average speed of 340·08 m.p.h., to win the Schneider Trophy outright for Britain in 1931. The Trophy, presented by a Frenchman in 1913 (when the winning speed was 45·75 m.p.h.), was open to seaplanes of all nations and was won at various times by Italy, Britain and the United States.

Stalin's Russia

Stalin transformed Russia by a second revolution, a revolution in production. In terms of human suffering, the cost was enormous, but the Soviet Union was changed from a backward agricultural country into an industrial giant.

△ **Stalin and Zhdanov at Kirov's funeral in 1934.** Many Communist leaders, including Bukharin and his friends, opposed Stalin's policies. By 1934, many Party members were ready to replace Stalin. Kirov was the most likely successor but, in December he was murdered. Stalin used the murder as an excuse to launch a series of purges to liquidate his enemies.

The dreaded NKVD (security police) executed prominent leaders, while thousands of lesser Party members were killed or sent to prison camps. Then, in 1937, 14 out of the 16 Soviet generals were arrested.

The disappearance of experienced men from industry and the Army became so serious that Stalin, as though to show it was not his fault, had Yezhov, head of the NKVD, executed.

The Stalin era commenced in 1927, the year in which he contrived to have Trotsky expelled from the Party. Thenceforward, as the most powerful figure in the Soviet Union, he was able to carry out his policy of "Socialism in one country".

Rejecting the old dream of world revolution, Stalin determined to turn Russia into a truly Communist state by means of a colossal programme of industrialization. Because he felt that the capitalist powers were certain to attack Russia, progress had to be explosively rapid. Nothing must be allowed to hinder the production of coal, oil, steel, electricity, timber, cement and machinery.

Targets were set in the First Five Year Plan (1928-33) and workers had to accept shortages of food, clothing and housing, with a poor standard of living, as the price of rewards in the future.

Farm production was all-important, not merely to feed the workers but also to pay for imported foreign machines with Russian grain. But the peasants, especially the better-off peasants known as *kulaks*, stuck to the capitalist practice of selling produce for a profit. Stalin decided to break them.

Collectivization (merging small holdings into large units in order to make use of farm machinery) was forced through. Some five million peasants who resisted were executed or left to die of starvation.

This drastic policy, along with rivalries inside the Party, aroused opposition to Stalin. Stalin replied with a most bloody purge of the Party, the Army and even his own N.K.V.D. (security police). All the surviving Bolshevik leaders perished. Two-thirds of the senior Army officers, hundreds of political leaders and eight million ordinary citizens were killed or sent to prison camps.

By 1937, Stalin's power was total. Millions had died, but he had created an industrial state strong enough to withstand Hitler's armies.

▽ **Sulphuric acid plant at Voskrensk, near Moscow,** under construction during the winter of 1931. The Five Year Plan came out in two drafts, a moderate one and an "optimal" one calling for faster rates of progress. Workers were exhorted to get the Five Year Plan completed in four years. Vast "kombinats", multi-industrial complexes, were built, containing several interdependent industries on one site.

Comparative economic growth

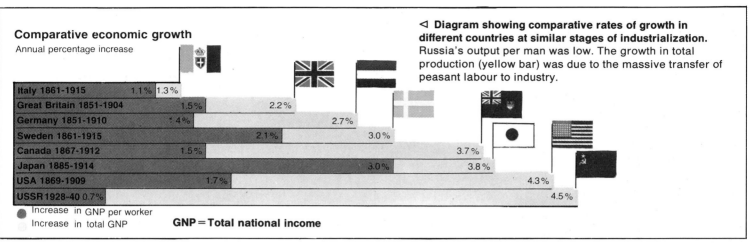

Annual percentage increase

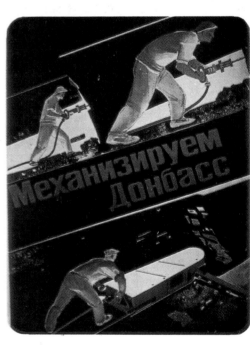

△ Diagram showing comparative rates of growth in different countries at similar stages of industrialization. Russia's output per man was low. The growth in total production (yellow bar) was due to the massive transfer of peasant labour to industry.

	Increase in GNP per worker	Increase in total GNP
Italy 1861-1915	1.1%	1.3%
Great Britain 1851-1904	1.5%	2.2%
Germany 1851-1910	1.4%	2.7%
Sweden 1861-1915	2.1%	3.0%
Canada 1867-1912	1.5%	3.7%
Japan 1885-1914	3.0%	3.8%
USA 1869-1909	1.7%	4.3%
USSR 1928-40	0.7%	4.5%

● Increase in GNP per worker
○ Increase in total GNP

GNP = Total national income

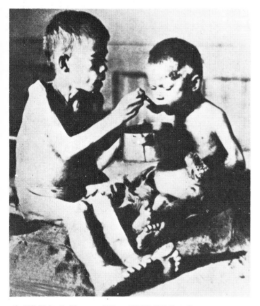

△ **Child victims of the 1932-33 famine,** caused by collectivization which disrupted agriculture, and by the Soviet government's insistence on exporting food to pay for foreign machinery.

△ **1931 poster** says state nursery schools will allow women to work in industry.

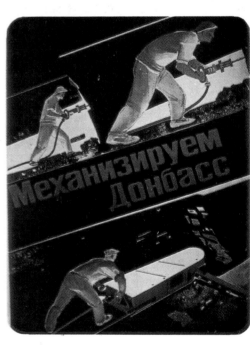

△ **Five Year Plan poster** proclaims progress in mining techniques.

Cars

During the thirties, cars acquired nearly all the features which are familiar to us today but, except in America, private motoring was still confined to the middle and upper classes.

As new types of steel could be pressed into more diverse shapes, car designers had greater scope and freedom. Bodies became less box-like and there was more concentration on curves and streamlining. Cars generally stood high, with more headroom and legroom for passengers than today, though there developed a craze for low lines, so that, in some cars, driver and passengers could scarcely see out.

Aided by better fuels, materials and design, engine performances improved. The Morris Cowley's 1500 cc. engine of the twenties, for instance, was replaced in 1932 by a 1292 cc. engine developing more power and using less fuel. "Balloon" tyres and independent suspension on front wheels gave a more comfortable ride. Bumpers came into widespread use, with direction indicators, the most popular type being a semaphore arm which clicked out from a metal case on the side of the body.

Safety glass was introduced for windscreens and the hand-operated screen-wiper gave way to an electric wiper usually set at the top of the screen.

Most bodies were the saloon or sedan type, closed in against the weather, but there was a demand for "sunshine" roofs, usually the sliding-panel type. The "Station Wagon" or "Estate Car" came on to the market as an all-purpose vehicle but most cars carried luggage on a steel rack fixed at the back of the car. Then came an extension of the body into a tail compartment called the "boot" or "trunk".

A notable advance occurred when Armstrong-Siddeley introduced a semi-automatic gear box, to be followed by the Daimler's Fluid Flywheel which did away with the clutch. By 1939, in America, Oldsmobiles and Cadillacs had been fitted with a fully automatic gear change known as the G.M. Hydramatic.

△ **Modern French** *Deux Chevaux* **Citroen.** First designed in 1937, the shape of the *Deux Chevaux* has changed remarkably little over the years, though early models had corrugated roofs. It was brought into production after World War Two, and it proved a cheap, sturdy car, with flexible suspension that absorbed even violent shock.

Like the Volkswagen "beetle" (see page 15) it shows how practical and durable car design had become by the late thirties.

▷ **Citroen 12,** 1935, a low, rakish and exceptionally strong car, built of pressed steel sections welded together. Its engine drove the front wheels, giving extra body space by eliminating the propeller-shaft.

▽ **Petrol advertisement of the thirties** when high-octane fuels improved speeds on roads and race tracks. Sports cars became popular, especially M.G. Midgets which won scores of hill-climbs, trials and track races.

▷ **Ford Eight,** 1935, a car produced for the English market. These appealed to people who wanted an economical car bigger than the baby Austin.

△ **Dodge car of 1937,** which shows how, by the late thirties, streamlining was an increasing feature of car design. The windscreen and bonnet slope back. The curve of the body is continued over the roof to the rear of the car, and the front and back mudguards emphasize the rounded contours.

△ **Morris Isis,** 1930, a low-priced English saloon. Its design shows the influence of the larger American cars of the late twenties. Still based on the square rather than the curve, it has an upright, box-like look.

△ **Austin Ten,** 1935, a later British family car, costing £175, unexciting but good value for money. Note the design: the windscreen and radiator have begun to slope backwards. Cars of this type had little appeal in America, where great distances, good roads and cheap fuel called for big cars, like the handsome Packard, Cadillac, La Salle and Lincoln.

Car Production — Figures in thousands

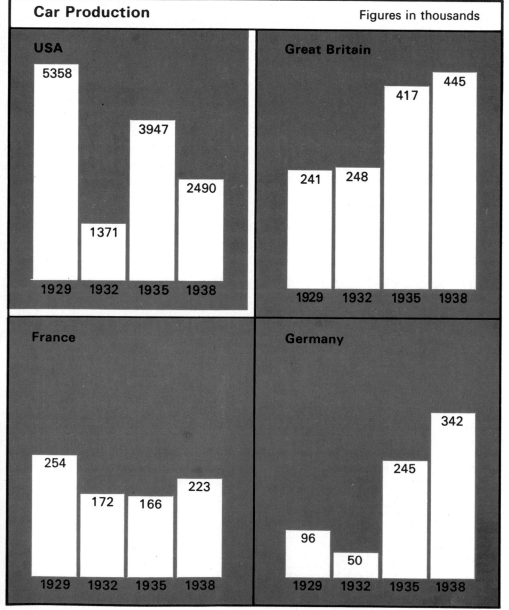

USA

1929	1932	1935	1938
5358	1371	3947	2490

Great Britain

1929	1932	1935	1938
241	248	417	445

France

1929	1932	1935	1938
254	172	166	223

Germany

1929	1932	1935	1938
96	50	245	342

△ **Diagram** showing how car production fell in the U.S. in 1932, one of the worst Depression years. British production remained remarkably stable, largely due to the enterprise of Morris and Austin.

△ **The multi-cylinder Cadillac V-16,** 1930, a smooth-running and luxurious car. The Cadillac firm belonged to the General Motors Company, a group which also included such famous names as Pontiac, Buick, Oldsmobile and Chevrolet.

Founded in 1908, General Motors first became really successful in the twenties, under the directorship of Alfred Sloan. By 1940, it had produced over 25 million cars. It is now the biggest motor firm in the world.

△ **Lincoln V-12,** 1934, a two-window town sedan. Lincoln was Ford's luxury marque. The V-12 cost over $3,000 and commanded 150 h.p. Like the Cadillac, it has the long lines, wide mudguards and wide running-board associated with the big American cars of the "gangster era".

Japan Goes to War

Many Japanese refer to the thirties as the "dark valley", the period when military fascists indulged in unchecked aggression abroad and murderous violence at home.

△ **German cartoon** depicting the Japanese attack on China. Japan maintained friendly relations with Nazi Germany.

Since World War One, Japan's population, industry, merchant navy and export trade had increased dramatically. But prices had soared, too. Extreme poverty existed alongside great wealth and the country experienced strikes, food riots, police persecution and political murders.

Japan's economy was badly hit by the Depression and, to the patriotic societies and groups of fanatical Army officers, the solution was obvious. Expansion into China would provide a vast market for Japanese goods.

When the thirties opened, the party in power favoured economic expansion without territorial conquest. This "soft" policy did not suit the extremists and, in November 1930, Prime Minister Hamaguchi was assassinated.

Manchuria, a northern province of China, rich in coal and minerals, had long been dominated by the Japanese. Their forces, known as the Kwantung Army, were stationed there, ostensibly to protect the mines and railways. In October 1931, Kwantung Army officers decided to forestall China's attempt to break the economic stranglehold. In defiance of their own government they seized the key town of Mukden and drove off the Chinese army.

In the following year, the Kwantung Army put the heir of the vanished Manchu dynasty, P'u Yi, on the throne of Manchuria, calling the puppet-state Manchukuo.

When the League of Nations condemned the creation of Manchukuo and called for the withdrawal of Japanese troops, Japan's delegates merely walked out of the League meeting.

In 1937, war spread into China itself, where Japanese troops captured Peking and Tientsin and moved south to take Shanghai and Nanking with terrible slaughter. The League protested, but could not prevent the capture of Hankow, Canton and Wuhan.

As Europe's own war approached in 1939, Japan controlled nearly all China's richest provinces and most of her coastline. Chiang Kai-shek, the Chinese generalissimo, had retreated to Chungking, far to the west, and seemed certain to negotiate or surrender. He did neither. In so vast an area, Japan's forces were thinly spread and Chinese guerillas could operate indefinitely. Chiang still held western China and he rightly believed that Japan must come into conflict with the United States. Then his war would be as good as won.

◁ **Poverty in a Tokyo slum.** Japan's capitalist system produced extremes of poverty and wealth; labour was plentiful and workers were poorly paid by the giant industrial companies. Farmers depended on production of rice for the home market and of raw silk for the United States. Prices dropped disastrously during the Depression years.

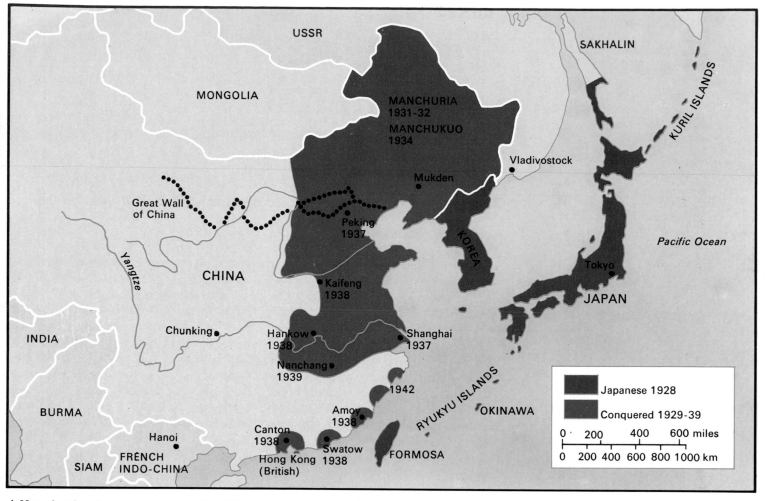

△ **Map showing Japanese expansion into China.** Japan itself was about the size of California with a population half that of the U.S., so, to the nationalists, expansion seemed essential. By 1939, Japanese forces had overrun much of eastern China from Peking to Canton.

▽ **A Japanese sentry on the Great Wall of China** looks across Japanese occupied territory. From Inner Mongolia, Japanese armies launched attacks southwards into China but, on the Russian border, they suffered a severe check at the hands of the Russian Marshal Zhukov.

China–The Long March

In 1934, rather than face extermination in the south, the Chinese Communists made an epic march to the north-west.

From 1928, Chiang Kai-shek's Nationalist government at Nanking was recognized as the legitimate government of China. Surviving Communists, under Chu Teh and Mao Tse-tung, had fled to the Hunan-Kiangsi provinces where they organized guerrilla warfare against the Nationalists.

In 1930, Chiang organized the first Bandit Extermination Campaign, but he failed to crush the guerrillas. Second, third and fourth campaigns were no more successful but, although the Japanese had seized Manchuria and had defeated Chinese troops at Shanghai, Chiang refused to call off the anti-Communist drive.

In the Fifth Campaign, he showed he had learned from past mistakes. Advised by German officers sent by Hitler, Chiang sealed off the Communist-held territory.

The Communists decided to break the blockade by leaving their bases in order to undertake the tremendous journey to Shensi province, a Communist stronghold in north-west China.

The Long March began in October 1934, when 100,000 Communists, with women and children, set off towards the western mountains. Other groups undertook separate marches to Shensi. Chiang's armies followed. They could not, however, catch up with the main forces which had to suffer more from hunger, snowstorms and terrible terrain than from enemy action.

After a year of appalling hardship, Mao reached Shensi. Less than a third of his army had survived. The other forces straggled in months later to raise the Red Army's strength to 80,000. The Long March had been an epic feat of courage and endurance but, for the time being, it seemed as if victory belonged to Chiang Kai-shek.

▽ **Nationalist troops** preparing to set out on one of the "extermination" campaigns. The heavily-laden mule-train indicates why they failed to defeat the nimble, elusive guerrillas. Mao described their tactics: "When the enemy attacks, we retreat; when he halts we harry him; when he retreats, we pursue."

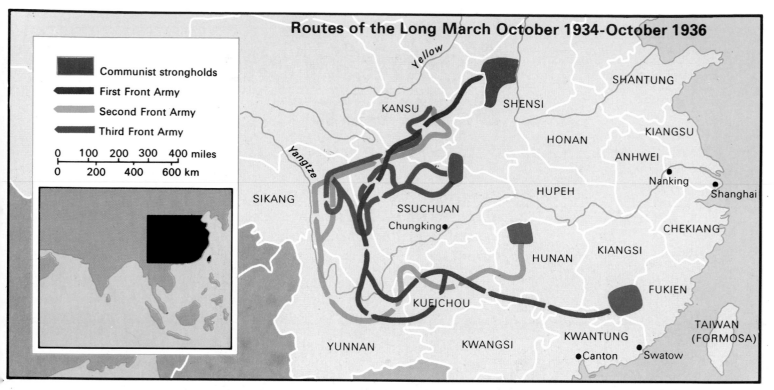

Routes of the Long March October 1934-October 1936

Legend:
- Communist strongholds
- First Front Army
- Second Front Army
- Third Front Army

0 100 200 300 400 miles
0 200 400 600 km

Map labels: Yellow, KANSU, SHENSI, SHANTUNG, KIANGSU, HONAN, ANHWEI, Nanking, Yangtze, SIKANG, SSUCHUAN, Chungking, HUPEH, Shanghai, CHEKIANG, HUNAN, KIANGSI, FUKIEN, KUEICHOU, KWANGSI, KWANTUNG, TAIWAN (FORMOSA), YUNNAN, Canton, Swatow

△ **Map showing the routes taken by the Communists.** Their worst suffering occurred when crossing the uninhabited region of Sikang. Ho Lung took a more southern and western route than Mao and he was the last to arrive, nearly a year afterwards. Chang Kuo-t'ao, who set out from Ssuchuan, joined forces with Mao but they disagreed and split up. Kuo defected later to the Nationalists.

◁ **Mao during the Battle of Loushan Pass,** 1935, when his army routed Chiang Kai-shek's forces. Chiang failed to bring the Red Army to a major engagement and his air force had scant success in bombing its columns.

Mao asserted his authority in the remote areas. Local warlords merely held on to the cities and allowed the marchers to cross the countryside unimpeded. The Communists won the peasants' support by their good behaviour and by paying for supplies, mules and porterage.

Electricity and Daily Life

Electricity has been one of the main technological advances of recent times. In the thirties, electrical power became widely available, transforming industry, entertainment and the home.

Faraday built the first electric motor in the 19th century, but, for many years, electric lighting and domestic gadgets were luxuries which only the rich could afford. Ordinary people heated their homes with coal and used gas or oil lights; industry relied largely on steam power and streets were dimly lit by gas.

Advance came in the 20th century with the building of power-stations in the more advanced countries and by the construction of national grids of transmission lines. By 1931, Charles Parsons' steam turbine had provided the world with vast quantities of electrical power.

Electricity became essential for many industrial processes, for driving machines and making machine-tools, for railways, cranes, lifts, collieries and rolling mills in the steel industry. The diesel-electric locomotive was a new source of power.

As early as 1920, the Ideal Home Exhibition in London had featured an all-electric house; its advantages were mainly electric light and heating. By the thirties, new houses were always wired for electricity, and older homes "went electric" if owners could afford the cost. All kinds of labour-saving devices became available, from cookers and washing machines to electric toasters and kettles. High streets and holiday resorts were transformed by the brilliance of shop window displays and illuminated buildings.

In Britain, output of electricity was seven times greater in 1938 than in 1920; Germany's output trebled in eleven years and Russia's rulers recognized that electrification was essential to a modern industrial state. By the thirties, electricity had become the measure of civilization.

△ **A 1905 vacuum cleaner,** one of the earliest models; it contained its own electric motor. The dust bag was connected to the front and the cleaning attachments to the top. At this time it was a novelty introduced into a few wealthy houses. There were plenty of maids to do the sweeping and dusting. By the thirties, convenient-size models were produced which could be plugged into electric sockets. **As the cartoon below shows,** they were mostly sold by energetic door-to-door salesmen.

"I tell you I don't want an electric cleaner!"

△ **Small batteries for torches** came into use by the time of World War One. This thirties advertisement proclaims their usefulness in a home not yet fitted with electric lighting.

△ **A "Genelex" electric washing machine** and wringer, manufactured in 1937. It took the drudgery out of wash-day for middle-class women but it was too expensive for most housewives. They washed by hand, using a wash-board and a hand-wringer.

BLACKPOOL / MASTERPIECE OF DAZZLING LIGHT

Come, share these glorious autumn joys.

SEP. 24th T
OCT. 24th, 193

△ **A poster advertising Blackpool,** one of the seaside resorts which made a feature of its ''illuminations''. Cheap electricity and mass-produced electric bulbs banished darkness from the world's towns and cities. Times Square, New York, and Piccadilly Circus, London, became famous for their neon advertisements. Streets were now lit by mercury vapour or sodium vapour lamps and fluorescent tubes began to appear in shops and offices. Flood-lighting of monuments and public buildings was a new attraction.

◁ **Man mastering electricity**—a mural by F. S. Bradford at the New York World Fair, 1939. This painting symbolizes man's new-found dominance over nature.

▽ **British television set, 1937:** the cathode-ray tube had to be mounted vertically with the screen facing upwards, so you looked at the picture in a mirror set in the lid. This set cost £63.

Invasion of Ethiopia

When Mussolini defeated Haile Selassie, he demonstrated the bankruptcy of the League of Nations.

△ **Emperor Haile Selassie,** greeted by a foreign delegate at his coronation in 1930. He introduced some reforms into his backward, semi-barbaric kingdom, but he had to contend with hostile feudal chiefs.

Ethiopia, or Abyssinia, as it was called, was a mountainous land so remote and poor that it had escaped the attention of the European empire-builders. What lay behind the Italian attack? The Italians felt they had been cheated by the Treaty of Versailles when they received not one of the former German colonies.

Ethiopia, the last sizeable area in Africa (apart from Liberia) without a colonial overlord, would enlarge the Italian Empire. Its conquest would also provide military glory for Mussolini's legions. The adventure would divert attention from discontent at home where the Fascist régime had run into difficulties. Furthermore, there was an old score to pay off. In 1898, the Ethiopians had wiped out an Italian army at Adowa. Mussolini declared that Adowa must be avenged.

The excuse came with a dispute over a tiny oasis called Wal Wal. The League of Nations postponed discussion of the incident, giving Mussolini time to assemble troops and stores in Eritrea and Italian Somaliland. Claiming that Ethiopia's "warlike aggressive spirit" had forced war on Italy, he launched the invasion in October 1935.

Even allowing for the incompetence of the Italian command, it was virtually impossible to fail against an enemy armed with spears and obsolete rifles. Aircraft, tanks and modern transport made the contest absurdly one-sided. It was remarkable only for the fact that the Italians took seven months to reach Addis Ababa, the capital.

The League had done worse than nothing. By imposing sanctions which did not include coal and oil, it enraged Mussolini without harming his war effort and made him look to Hitler for friendship. No country was prepared to take up arms on Haile Selassie's behalf and he went into dignified exile.

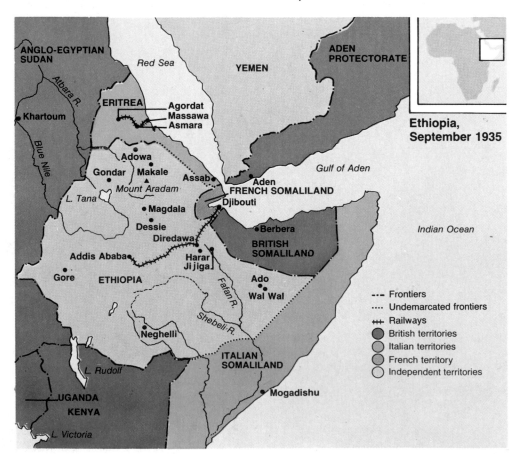

Ethiopia, September 1935

- -- Frontiers
- ···· Undemarcated frontiers
- +++ Railways
- Ⓐ British territories
- Ⓐ Italian territories
- Ⓐ French territory
- Ⓐ Independent territories

△ **Enthusiastic Italian troops** display portraits of *Il Duce* (Mussolini) from their troopship.

◁ **Map of Ethiopia:** the Italians launched their invasion from Eritrea and Italian Somaliland. While General Graziani advanced from Mogadishu, the incompetent Bono took so long capturing Adowa that he was replaced by General Badoglio, who entered Addis Ababa on May 5, 1936.

LA DOMENICA DEL CORRIERE

NEL REGNO	ESTERO		
Anno . . . . . . L. 15,-	L. 30,-	**Si pubblica a Milano ogni settimana**	Uffici del giornale : Via Solferino, 28 - Milano
Semestre . . . . . » 8,-	» 16,-		

Per le inserzioni rivolgersi all'Amministrazione del *Corriere della Sera* - Via Solferino, 28 - Milano.

Supplemento illustrato del "Corriere della Sera"

Per tutti gli articoli e illustrazioni è riservata la proprietà letteraria e artistica, secondo le leggi e i trattati internazionali.

Anno XXXVIII — N. 6   9 Febbraio 1936 - Anno XIV   Centesimi 30 la copia

Le Camicie Nere al passo di Uarieu. I militi della Divisione XXVIII Ottobre, dopo aver resistito per due giorni agli assalti delle truppe scelte dei ras Cassa e Sejum, attaccano alla baionetta sbaragliando definitivamente gli assalitori. (Disegno di A. Beltrame).

Italian newspaper showing Blackshirt troops in action against the Ethiopians. Besides bombs and tanks, the Italians used poison-gas.

Democracies and Dictatorships

Backwardness, poverty and economic chaos caused many Europeans to lose faith in parliamentary democracy. Dictators seized power, usually with dire results.

In a democracy, people possess freedoms which dictators nearly always deny. These include freedom to vote for any party, freedom to speak, to read, to join a union and to oppose the government. The democratic way of life is neither easy nor particularly efficient. It calls for honest politicians and officials, and it requires a nation which trusts and understands the system.

After World War One, nearly a dozen new states came into existence in central and eastern Europe. Few of them, except perhaps Poland and some Balkan countries, had had experience of parliamentary government and citizens' rights. Most were economically and educationally backward, with large peasant populations and national minorities. Democratic government was not likely to transform society and bring prosperity to these countries overnight. Yet that had been the hope and, in disappointment, it was easy to become contemptuous of democracy.

As we have seen, fear of Communism played a big part in bringing the dictatorships of Germany and Italy to power. It had a similar effect on the traditional ruling classes in the new states.

When the Depression threw frail economies into chaos, democracy seemed to have failed. Would-be dictators or military cliques emerged to take power on promises to bring authority and order to public affairs.

In the older democracies, Britain, France, Holland, Sweden, Belgium and Spain (until 1939), parliamentary government survived. It perished in Germany, Italy and the new States, except Czechoslovakia.

The dictatorships varied. Hitler and Mussolini stood on bases of mass popular support. King Boris of Bulgaria, King Carol of Rumania, King Alexander of Yugoslavia and General Metaxas and King George of Greece relied on small military groups, Court followers and property owners. Poland's war-hero Pilsudski and Austria's Dr Dollfuss were not Fascists so much as authoritarian rulers trying to bring stability to their countries. The lesser dictatorships failed because they lacked the basis of real power.

△ **Member of Rumania's Iron Guard,** wearing a swastika arm-band. King Carol used this terrorist organization to win dictatorial power and then butchered its leaders.

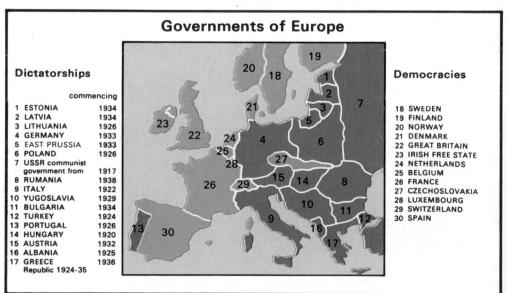

Governments of Europe

Dictatorships

		commencing
1	ESTONIA	1934
2	LATVIA	1934
3	LITHUANIA	1926
4	GERMANY	1933
5	EAST PRUSSIA	1933
6	POLAND	1926
7	USSR communist government from	1917
8	RUMANIA	1938
9	ITALY	1922
10	YUGOSLAVIA	1929
11	BULGARIA	1934
12	TURKEY	1924
13	PORTUGAL	1926
14	HUNGARY	1920
15	AUSTRIA	1932
16	ALBANIA	1925
17	GREECE	1936
	Republic 1924-35	

Democracies

18	SWEDEN
19	FINLAND
20	NORWAY
21	DENMARK
22	GREAT BRITAIN
23	IRISH FREE STATE
24	NETHERLANDS
25	BELGIUM
26	FRANCE
27	CZECHOSLOVAKIA
28	LUXEMBOURG
29	SWITZERLAND
30	SPAIN

△ **Map of Europe** showing that the dictatorships, with the exception of Portugal (Salazar was its ruler), lay in Central and Eastern Europe. The West and Czechoslavakia clung to democracy and, in most cases, to constitutional monarchy.

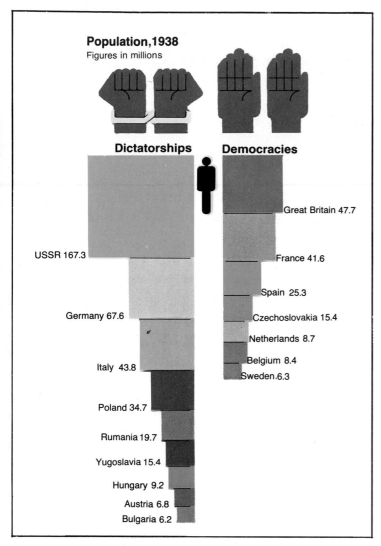

Population, 1938
Figures in millions

Dictatorships **Democracies**

USSR 167.3

Great Britain 47.7

France 41.6

Germany 67.6

Spain 25.3

Czechoslovakia 15.4

Netherlands 8.7

Italy 43.8

Belgium 8.4

Sweden 6.3

Poland 34.7

Rumania 19.7

Yugoslavia 15.4

Hungary 9.2

Austria 6.8

Bulgaria 6.2

△ **Diagram showing** comparative sizes of some European democracies and dictatorships. Most people lived under a dictatorship.

△ **Italian stamp showing Mussolini** in a heroic pose. Europe's first Fascist, he extended a friendly hand to Hitler, though he feared the take-over of Austria. The Western democracies' hostility, however feeble, to the Ethiopian invasion drove the two dictators together.

◁ **Marshal Pilsudski,** the Polish hero and patriot. He over-threw the Polish government by a military coup d'état in 1926 and ruled for the next nine years as a dictator. Without abolishing opposition parties, he used his power, sometimes brutally, to prevent them having any in-fluence. After his death in 1935, a military clique ruled the country.

△ **A rally of Action Française,** the nationalistic French monarchist movement, is dispersed by Paris police, May 1934. Fascist forces took part in street fighting with the Left. Stalin, worried by the prospect of a Fascist government in France, ordered the Communists to form a Popular Front with the Socialists. Léon Blum became head of the Socialist government in 1936, but the Communists refused support and the Popular Front gradually fell apart. Nonetheless, democracy survived in France.

△ **Austrian stamp with portrait of Dr Dollfuss.** He became Chancellor in 1932, when Austria's economy was in ruins. The country was torn by violent hostility between the Heimwehr (Right-wing defence force) and the Schutzbund (Socialist league).

Dollfuss assumed dictatorial powers, with support from Roman Catholics, the Heimwehr and Mussolini, but was opposed by the Socialists and Austrian Nazis. He banned both parties and attacked the workers' flats in Vienna with artillery. But his power was precarious and the Nazis murdered him in 1934.

The Spanish Civil War

△ **Spanish Republican poster,** 1936, jeers at the Nationalist forces which include Moroccans, a German, an Italian and the Roman Catholic Church.

In Spain, Franco's strength was based principally in the Army, the middle-classes, the Catholics, and the Carlists, an old-established patriotic monarchist group, strong in the rural north. There was a growing Fascist Party (the Falange) which also supported Franco's military conspiracy against the government.

What began as a purely Spanish affair became a struggle between Fascism and Communism, involving all Europe.

When the Spanish elections of February 1936 returned a Republican government of the Left, disorders broke out that led to civil war. The Republicans or Loyalists, comprised Liberals, Socialists, Communists, Anarchists and others. They had actually polled fewer votes than the Right-wing groups, who saw their way of life and their religion threatened by this narrow victory.

In July, a military rising occurred in Spanish Morocco, led by General Franco, who transferred his forces to the mainland of Spain and rapidly won control in the south and the north-west. He set up a new government in Burgos, while the Republicans moved their government headquarters to Barcelona. In the fighting that followed, both sides behaved with appalling ferocity.

None of the major Powers could remain indifferent. The French prime minister, Blum, would have liked to send French help to the Republicans, but opposition in his cabinet and the British attitude caused him to hold back. Britain persuaded France, Germany, Italy and Russia to agree not to take part in the Civil War. The dictators had no intention of keeping their promises.

Hitler sent planes, tanks, pilots and technicians because victory for Franco would embarrass France. The war also offered opportunities to try out new tactics and to test young German pilots. Mussolini, happy to see Italy playing a role in Europe, sent 60,000 troops to assist Franco. In response to world-wide Communist pleas, Stalin despatched men and materials to the Republicans.

Russian aid eventually dwindled to a trickle and, although Left-wing supporters from many countries fought valiantly in the International Brigade, German-Italian aid to Franco was decisive. In January 1939, he captured Barcelona and when Madrid fell soon afterwards, the war was over. Franco and the forces of the Right ruled Spain for more than thirty years.

Map 1 (July 1936):
FRANCE
•Corunna
•Vigo
•Burgos
•Valladolid
•Salamanca
•Madrid
PORTUGAL
SPAIN
•Cordoba
•Seville
•Cadiz
Franco's Nationalist Forces
Areas gained   Areas occupied
July 1936

Map 2 (March 1937):
San Sebastian
ASTURIAS   BASQUE PROVINCES
•Madrid   •Teruel
•Toledo
•Badajoz
Granada
Malaga
Gibraltar
March 1937

Map 3 (December 1938):
Bilbao
Santander   Guernica
•Madrid
December 1938

Map 4 (February 1939):
CATALONIA
Tarragona•   •Barcelona
•Madrid
February 1939

Map 5 (March 1939):
Guadalajara
Madrid
Albacete   •Valencia
•Alicante
Cartagena
Almeria
March 1939

△ **Progress of the war:** at the outset, Franco seemed certain to lose, for the industrial towns, Madrid and two-thirds of the country were against him. However, with foreign help and thanks to disunity between the various Left-wing groups, he made steady progress in 1937, but failed to take Madrid and was checked at Teruel. In 1938, he broke through to the east coast, overran Catalonia, the government stronghold, and captured Barcelona in January 1939. This was virtually the end. The Republicans began to fight among themselves, their leaders fled abroad. In April, Franco declared the war over.

▽ **Silhouetted against the sky, Republican troops** go into action against Franco's army. The Republicans included every shade of Left-wing opinion, from Liberals to Anarchists, from intellectuals to urban workers and peasants.

They were joined by many Socialists who became disgusted by quarrels in their own party. Communists organized the International Brigade in which British, Americans and Frenchmen fought for the Republican cause. The British Labour Party, normally peace-loving, wanted to intervene on the Republican side.

The Artist and Society

The twenties had been an era of experiment, but the menacing events of the thirties pressed hard on artists.

Much of the writing and painting of this period expressed the impact of Communism, Fascism, unemployment and human suffering.

Communism exercised an especially powerful fascination. Brecht, the German writer, Jean-Paul Sartre and Malraux, the French novelists, W. H. Auden, Stephen Spender and Cecil Day-Lewis, the trio of young English poets, and George Orwell, all became Communists, or Communist sympathizers. They saw in the Soviet Union a new hope for humanity. Some of them served in the Spanish Civil War, and the struggle produced books like Hemingway's *For Whom The Bell Tolls*, Orwell's *Homage to Catalonia*, Malraux's *Days of Hope* and some poems.

Fiction and documentary writing were marked by a concern for social conditions and for the ordinary man's agonized bewilderment. There was the German Hans Fallada's *Little Man, What Now?*, Orwell's account of his life as one of the unemployed, *The Road To Wigan Pier*, and the French writer Céline's grim account of poverty in Paris. Graham Greene's *Brighton Rock* looked keenly at a seedy aspect of English life, while, in *The Grapes of Wrath*, Steinbeck drew a harrowing picture of the plight of American "Okies" in the dust bowl.

China was in the news—Edgar Snow's *Red Star Over China* described the civil war, and Pearl S. Buck's *The Good Earth* became a best-seller. Louis Golding's *Magnolia Street* and Clifford Odets' play *Awake and Sing* showed what it was like to be a poor Jew in England and New York. Sherwood's play *Idiot's Delight* (1936) prophesied the outbreak of World War Two.

△ **Leni Riefenstahl,** German film-director, making her pro-Nazi film of the 1936 Berlin Olympics. Many German artists, however, opposed the régime. Some, like the playwright Brecht, were forced into exile.

◁ **George Orwell** (1903-50), who served in the Spanish Civil War and became disgusted with Russian Communism. Later books (*Animal Farm* and *1984*) describe the horrors of totalitarianism.

▷ **Cover of French pamphlet,** *Help Spain,* by the Spanish artist, Miro. Another expatriate, and Republican, Picasso, painted pictures exposing the horrors of the war, including the bombing of Guernica. the Basque capital.

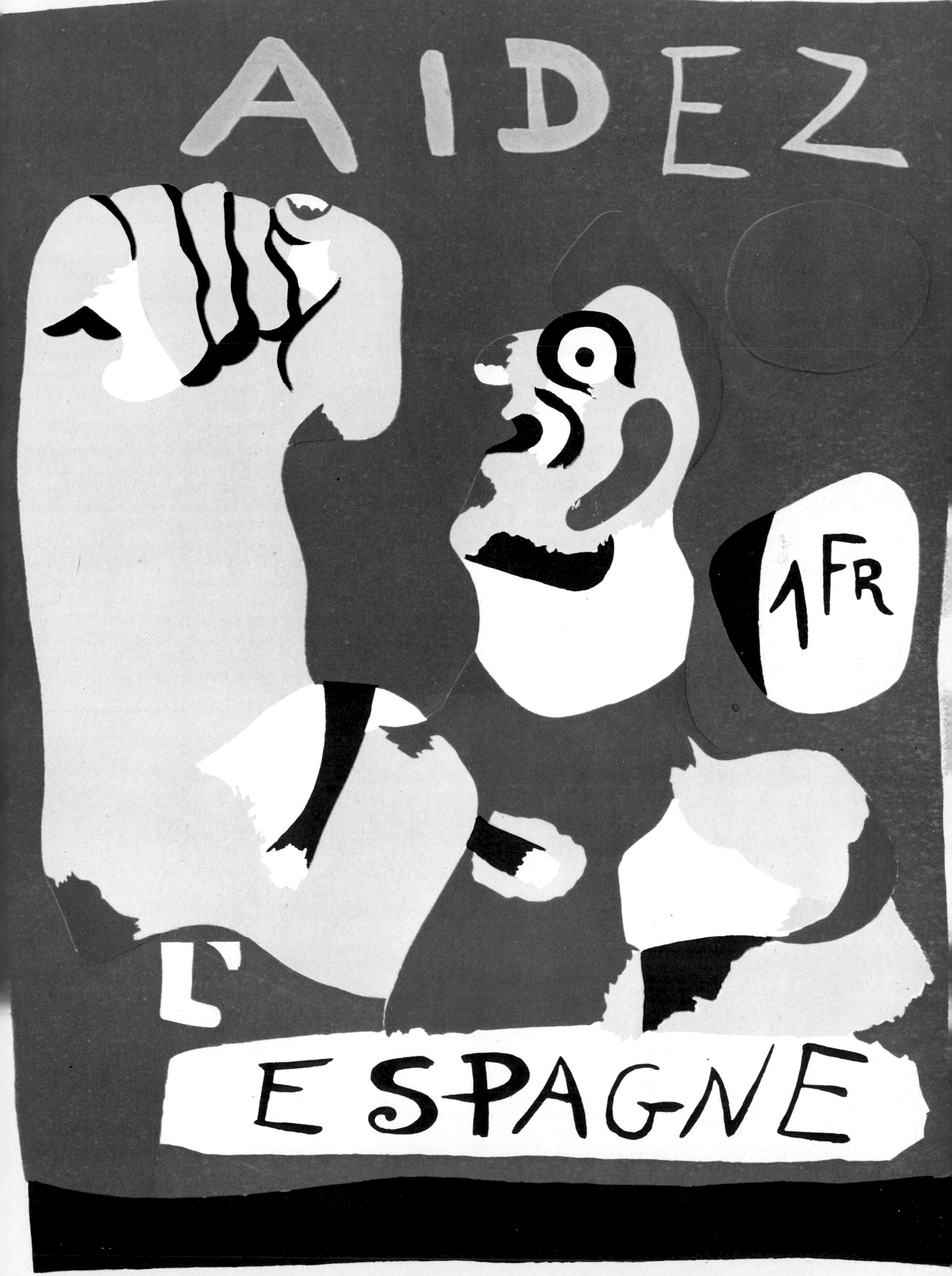
AIDEZ
1 FR
L'
ESPAGNE

Cinema

The talkies brought in the film industry's Golden Age of super-cinemas, packed audiences and lavish productions.

This was the time when some 40 per cent of the population of Britain and America went to the cinema every week and 25 per cent went twice or more often. Nearly all the films they saw were made in Hollywood.

Britain, France, Italy and Germany possessed their own film industries which turned out some notable films, like the British *Blackmail* and *The Private Life of Henry VIII*, the German *Blue Angel* and the French *Harvest* and *Le Million*. But they could not rival Hollywood's mammoth production of nearly 600 films a year.

No other industry could boast such extraordinary growth in one generation as the American film industry. All trace of the amateurism of the silent days had vanished and, in technical skill and entertainment, Hollywood films remained almost unchallenged. No other country could have produced the great epics of the decade, *Gone With The Wind*, and *The Sign of The Cross*, nor the lavish musicals and full-length cartoons.

Few of Hollywood's films dealt with mankind's problems; the cinema was a place of refuge, a glamour palace where people could enter a world of song and dance, comedy, and adventure. The most glamorous vamp of the era was Jean Harlow, the "blonde bombshell".

The talkies also brought a new kind of star. Katherine Hepburn, Spencer Tracy, Bing Crosby, Ginger Rogers, and Judy Garland were just nice folk who happened to be actors and actresses. An interesting development was the permanence of the screen favourites. Many of the idols, whether homely, like Tracy, exotic, like Garbo and Dietrich, or comic, like the Marx Brothers, went on making pictures for years and years. They were old friends whom people wanted to go on seeing.

△ **King Kong,** the monster who only wanted to be loved, from the film of the same name, 1933. Two other fantasy horror-films, *Dracula* and *Frankenstein,* were classics of their kind. More realistic thrillers, like *Confessions of a Nazi Spy* and *Beasts of Berlin,* were openly anti-Hitler.

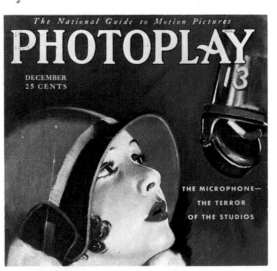

△ **Film magazine cover** showing a star of the silent films, Norma Talmadge, gazing apprehensively at a microphone. Sound films destroyed some of the silent stars, because their voices were unsuitable or because the talkies called for a more natural style of acting. Speech inevitably disclosed an actor's class and nationality and most of the big stars of the thirties were distinctively American —Clark Gable, Spencer Tracy and Robert Taylor, for example.

△ **Charlie Chaplin** in *City Lights,* 1931. Chaplin's style was perfectly suited to mime, so, in this film and *Modern Times* (1936), he remained silent, long after the introduction of sound.

△ **Poster** showing two of the big stars of the thirties, Ronald Colman and Claudette Colbert in one of the glamorous adventure films of the time. Like Charles Boyer (French) and Leslie Howard (English), these foreigners often starred in roles considered too exotically romantic for Americans.

△ **Fred Astaire,** who starred with Ginger Rogers in a number of successful musicals. Apart from their dancing skill, their exuberance and humour, the catchy songs and lavish sets of their films provided a marvellous kind of escapism.

△ *Snow White and the Seven Dwarfs,* Walt Disney's first feature-length cartoon in colour. He had made his name with Mickey Mouse and moved on to this more ambitious cartoon, released in 1938.

The public loved it and clamoured for more, but cartoon-making was a slow, costly process and *Pinocchio,* his next, took two years to complete. Another feature cartoon of 1938 was *Gulliver's Travels* but it could not approach Disney's standards.

△ **Shirley Temple** was *the* child star of the decade. Her cute personality endeared her to millions of sentimental cinemagoers. Her only rivals were two boy-actors, Mickey Rooney and Freddie Bartholomew.

△ **Marlene Dietrich,** as Lola, displays her famous legs in *The Blue Angel.* A German film made in 1930, it describes a professor who sets out to denounce a night-club performer for leading his students astray and is himself ruined by her. French and German films displayed greater realism than most Hollywood productions but, when the Nazis came in, the best German producers fled. Chaplin, the Marx Brothers, Laurel and Hardy and Shirley Temple were all banned by Goebbels.

1938: Year of Munich

Those who welcomed the Munich Agreement felt that it stood for the triumph of commonsense. Conciliation was better than war. Its opponents (and they were few in 1938) saw it as the surrender of France and Britain to fear.

In March 1938, German tanks entered Vienna and Hitler announced, in defiance of the Treaty of Versailles, the union of Germany and Austria. France and Britain did nothing, though the union, known as the *Anschluss*, made Czechoslovakia vulnerable.

The spotlight fell upon the Sudetenland. This was an area of Czechoslovakia containing three million German-speaking inhabitants, a discontented minority whose leaders demanded union with Germany. Hitler encouraged them, but Dr Benes, President of Czechoslovakia felt sure he could rely on the protection of France and Britain. Indeed, Daladier, the French premier, declared that France would fight if the Czechs were attacked. Chamberlain, the British Prime Minister, refused to join him in issuing a warning to Hitler. He believed that the best way to keep peace was to give the Germans what they wanted.

All that summer, the Sudeten question was kept on the boil. In September, Chamberlain flew to Germany for urgent discussions with Hitler. As a result, Britain and France informed Benes he must hand over all areas with a German-speaking population of over 50 per cent. Benes bravely refused, whereupon Hitler stepped up his demands; the French Army and the British Fleet began to mobilize and the Czechs stood ready to fight.

It seemed as if Hitler's bluff had been called. But he sensed that Britain and France would not fight for Czechoslovakia. So he pushed on to the brink, uttering threats and abuse until war appeared certain. Once again, Chamberlain intervened to call a Four Power meeting at Munich to settle the Sudeten problem. On 30 September, Hitler, Daladier, Mussolini and Chamberlain agreed on the areas which were to be handed over at once. The Czechs were not even consulted. Their country was betrayed.

△ **Swiss comment on Munich:** the flag of peace hides a field-gun. Some believed peace was secured, but Munich destroyed Czechoslovakia and brought Hitler a rich haul of arms.

△ **Hitler signs the Munich Agreement.** The other signatories were Mussolini, Daladier and Chamberlain.

△ **Map of Czechoslovakia,** showing the Sudetenland, handed over to Germany in 1938, and the smaller areas seized by Poland and Hungary. The Sudetenland was ceded with all its modern fortifications and weapons.

Czech defences were ruined. There was to be a "guarantee" of new frontiers, but when, in March 1939, German troops occupied Prague, neither Britain nor France took action. Independent Czechoslovakia ceased to exist.

△ **Berlin crowds welcome Hitler on his return from Munich.** He is said to have been disgusted by their enthusiasm for peace. Germans were glad that the *Führer* had brought their kinsmen, the Sudeten Germans, into the Reich, but few of them, including the Army High Command, wanted war. But Munich strengthened the Nazi fanatics. Once again, Hitler had proved himself more knowing and daring than the generals. Germany—and Italy, too—were drawn along in his wake.

△ **French army reservists in Paris drink to peace.** The French were overwhelmed with relief. War seemed to have been averted by a miracle. Later came realization that Czechoslovakia had been betrayed. Frantic preparations for war were made.

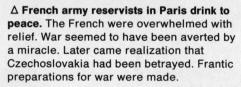

◁ **Epilogue to Munich:** anguish on the faces of the Czechs as German troops occupy Prague in March 1939. After Munich, there had been disputes in Czechoslovakia, where the premier of Slovakia was dismissed. He appealed to Hitler who summoned President Hacha to Berlin (Benes had gone into exile) and browbeat him into placing his country under German "protection"

Bohemia-Moravia were annexed to Germany, Slovakia became a protectorate. Ruthenia was given to Hungary. As Hitler delightedly announced, Czechoslovakia no longer existed.

Chamberlain was taken aback by the anger of the British people who at last realized they had been duped. Britain and France announced they would resist aggression in the Netherlands, Belgium and Switzerland. Moreover, Britain would stand by France in support of Poland with whom Hitler was already picking a quarrel.

The Outbreak of War

Oslo
NORWAY
Stockholm
SWEDEN
DENMARK
Copenhagen
NORTH SEA
EIRE   BRITAIN
London
Amsterdam
NETHERLANDS
Brussels
BELGIUM
Wilhelmshaven   Elbe   Berlin   Oder
GERMANY
Rhine
LUXEMBOURG
Seine   Paris
MAGINOT
LINE   SIEGFRIED
LINE
FRANCE
Munich
Berchtesgaden
Berne   Innsbruck
SWITZERLAND
Geneva
Milan
ITALY
Nice
Corsica
SPAIN
MEDITERRANEAN   SEA
Rome

BALTIC   SEA
Tallinn   ESTONIA
Riga   LATVIA
LITHUANIA   Kaunas
Memel
Gdynia   Konigsberg
Danzig   EAST PRUSSIA
Bromberg
(Bydgoszcz)   Warsaw
POLAND   RUSSIA
Vistula   UKRAINE
Prague
Sudetenland   CZECHOSLOVAKIA
Danube
Vienna
Budapest
HUNGARY
RUMANIA
Bucharest
Belgrade   Danube
YUGOSLAVIA
BULGARIA
Sofia
ALBANIA
Tirana   GREECE   TURKEY
ADRIATIC   SEA
BLACK SEA

0   100   200
Miles

△ **Map:** Germany is poised to invade Poland, for the non-aggression pact with Russia has given Hitler a free hand (he feels certain that France and Britain will back down). Stalin can grab the Baltic States and push his frontier forward by occupying eastern Poland.

▷ **How the nations stood in 1939:** Britain and France were pledged to act together, though France was now a rather hesitant partner. Their alliances with Poland and Turkey were practically useless. Britain and the United States stood on friendly terms, but there was no prospect of America declaring war. Mussolini had warned Hitler that Italy was not ready and would require vast quantities of materials.

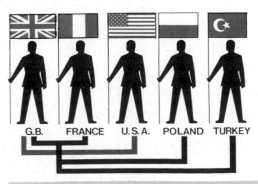

G.B.   FRANCE   U.S.A.   POLAND   TURKEY

GERMANY   ITALY   U.S.S.R.

Alliance ▬▬▬   Understanding
or Common Policy ▬▬▬   Non-Aggression
Pact ▬▬▬

48

Could the war which began on 1 September 1939, have been averted? Was its outbreak due to Polish obstinacy, to British blundering or to Hitler's unappeasable aggression?

1 September 1939, police and soldiers remove the customs barrier as Danzig becomes German.

After Munich, there was just one grievance left over from Versailles. The Polish Corridor separated East Prussia from Germany. Danzig, with a German population, was a Free City whose inhabitants were clamouring to be taken into the Fatherland.

Hitler was determined to settle the Polish question, which meant of course that Danzig must be handed over, along with a right of way through the Corridor. The Poles were informed of this in March 1939 and Colonel Beck, their Foreign Minister, replied with a blank "No". Nor did he consult the Western Powers, knowing that they sympathized with Germany over Danzig and would urge concession.

Chamberlain's reaction was astounding. On 31 March, he gave Poland a guarantee of support against aggression, ignoring the fact that it would be impossible to render any assistance, unless Britain was on friendly terms with Russia. Nevertheless, he must have thought that the guarantee, backed by France, would bring Hitler to his senses. In fact, Hitler told his generals to prepare to attack Poland in September and, for the moment, he repeated his demands for a settlement over Danzig.

Britain's next move was a belated approach to Russia for an "understanding" rather than a firm alliance.

Discussion was dragging on half-heartedly when a bombshell exploded. With horrified disbelief, the world learnt that Germany and Russia had signed a non-aggression pact! The Nazi and Communist dictators had come together.

Britain at once concluded an Anglo-Polish treaty, but it was certain that Poland must give way over Danzig. France and Britain certainly wanted her to do so, but Beck still refused. On 1 September 1939, Hitler ordered the attack.

Two days later, to honour the treaty she had made, Britain declared war on Germany and France followed suit.

The Main Events: 1930-1939

While America pursued domestic recovery, Europe and the Far East experienced a succession of crises. We can now see that, despite the League of Nations, non-aggression pacts, treaties and appeasements, these crises led inevitably to World War Two.

△ **1930:** King Carol of Rumania in Bucharest with his son, Prince Michael, after he returned from exile to take the throne.

△ **1932:** Roosevelt shakes hands with a farm-worker during his Presidential campaign.

△ **Berlin 1933:** Nazis force Communists to board a truck bound for a concentration camp.

1930

March: Gandhi encouraging civil disobedience in India. Unemployed riot in New York.
April: London Naval Treaty between Britain, U.S., Japan.
May: Gandhi imprisoned.
June: French troops evacuate Rhineland. Carol II becomes King of Rumania.
August: President Leguia of Peru overthrown. Pilsudski becomes dictatorial Prime Minister of Poland.
September: Nazis win 107 seats in Reichstag. Uriburu, President of Argentina.
October: Vargas becomes ruler of Brazil.
November: Premier Hamaguchi of Japan assassinated.
General
Allied occupation of Germany is ended.
Widespread disorder in Latin America.
De Rivera's dictatorship ends in Spain.
Collectivization of farms in Russia.
Airship *R101* crashes; Amy Johnson flies to Australia; Wiley Post flies round the world in 8 days 16 hours.
Slum clearance in Britain.
Haile Selassie crowned emperor of Ethiopia.
The Arts
Literature: Eliot *Ash Wednesday*; Maugham *Cakes and Ale*.
Music: Bartok, Holst, Stravinsky, Shostakovich; B.B.C. Symphony Orchestra founded.
Painters: Dufy, Klee, Picasso, Matisse, Roualt.
Cinema: Dietrich, *The Blue Angel*.

1932

January: Japanese troops attack Shanghai.
February: De Valera becomes President of the Irish Free State. Japan sets up puppet state of Manchukuo.
April: Germany's unemployed number more than six million. Hindenburg defeats Hitler in election for President.
May: Dollfuss becomes Chancellor of Austria. Chaco War begins between Bolivia and Paraguay.
July: Ottawa Conference to arrange "imperial preference", special trade agreements in the British Empire.
Nazis win 230 seats in the Reichstag.
Salazar becomes virtual dictator of Portugal.
August: J. Mollison flies Atlantic in 30 hours.
November: F. D. Roosevelt elected President of the U.S.
General
Britain abandons Free Trade; engages in economic war with Ireland.
Mosley founds British Union of Fascists.
Scientists make progress in atomic research.
Germans begin to build autobahns.
Sydney Harbour Bridge completed.
The Arts
Literature: Caldwell, *Tobacco Road*; Golding, *Magnolia Street*; Hemingway, *Death in the Afternoon*; Huxley, *Brave New World*.
Painters: Burra, Derain, Grant Still.
Cinema: *Shanghai Express*. Disney's *Silly Symphonies*.

1931

April: King Alphonso quits Spain.
May: Austria's leading bank fails.
June: Republican-Socialist government elected in Spain.
July: Bank failures and mounting unemployment in Germany.
August: Financial crisis in Britain; Labour government resigns.
September: Mukden incident; Japanese troops invade Manchuria. Gandhi attends conference in London.
October: General election in Britain; National Government wins enormous majority. Macdonald Prime Minister.
December: Statute of Westminster; British Dominions become sovereign states under the Crown.
General
World Depression has catastrophic effect on European economy. Unemployed number nearly three million in Britain. Chiang Kai-shek tries vainly to exterminate Communists.
First outside television broadcast.
Britain wins Schneider Trophy outright.
Electric razor invented.
The Arts
Literature: Buck, *The Good Earth*; O'Neill, *Morning becomes Electra*; Guedella, *The Duke*.
Theatre: Coward, *Cavalcade*.
Cinema: Chaplin, *City Lights*; Karloff, *Frankenstein*.
Painters: Dali, Chagall, Utrillo.
Music: Ravel, Walton.

1933

January: Hitler becomes Chancellor of Germany. Widespread riots in Spain.
February: Reichstag fire blamed on Communists.
March: Hitler secures Enabling Act to make laws without reference to the Reichstag. Roosevelt introduces his New Deal policy. Tennessee Valley Authority created. Japan withdraws from the League of Nations.
June: World Economic Conference in London fails. Dollfuss suppresses Austrian Nazi Party.
August: Batista becomes dictator of Cuba.
October: Germany leaves League of Nations. Chiang Kai-shek launches fifth campaign against Chinese Communists.
December: Prohibition repealed in the U.S.
General
Germany becomes totalitarian state. Opposition parties suppressed, concentration camps start.
Stalin begins purge of Soviet Communist Party.
Second Russian Five Year Plan.
U.S. establishes diplomatic relations with U.S.S.R.
Unrest in Spain, Fascist party formed.
Byrd's second Antarctic expedition.
The Arts
Literature: Spender, *Poems*; Hilton, *Lost Horizon*; James Thurber.
Music: Stravinsky, Kodaly, Ashton (ballet).
Cinema: Laughton, *The Private Life of Henry VIII*.
Painters: Matisse, Nash.

1934

January: Non-aggression treaty between Germany and Poland.
February: Paris riots over Stavisky affair, a shady financier said to have had dealings with French politicians. Dollfuss attacks workers' flats in Vienna.
June: Hitler and Mussolini meet in Venice. Night of the Long Knives; German S.A. destroyed.
July: Dollfuss murdered by Austrian Nazis. Cardenas becomes President of Mexico.
August: Death of Hindenburg. Hitler becomes President. German army swears allegiance.
September: Russia joins League of Nations.
October: King Alexander of Yugoslavia assassinated in Marseilles. Communist Long March begins in China.
December: Treason trials in Russia.
General
New Deal legislation introduces economic and social reforms in U.S.
Boris of Bulgaria sets up dictatorship.
Scott and Black fly England—Australia in 2 days 23 hours.
South Africa declares independence.
The Arts
Literature: Graves, *I, Claudius*; O'Hara, *Appointment in Samarra*.
Painters: Kandinsky, Klee; Picasso, *Bull-fight*.
Music: Shostakovich.

1935

January: France (Pierre Laval) makes agreement with Italy over Italian claims in Africa.
February: Saar plebiscite. Saar returned to Germany.
March: Hitler introduces conscription; announces formation of a German army.
April: Stresa Conference: Britain, France, Italy try to establish common front against Germany.
May: Franco-Russian-Czech defensive alliance. Pilsudski dies. Colonels take over in Poland.
June: Baldwin succeeds Macdonald as British Prime Minister.
August: Government of India Act; increased power to provincial governments; opposed by Congress. Social Security Act passed in U.S.
October: Italians invade Ethiopia.
November: League votes sanctions against Italy.
December: Samuel Hoare resigns as British Foreign Secretary, for his part in Hoare-Laval Pact offering huge gains in Ethiopia to Italy.
General
Acute tension in Europe. Jews persecuted in Germany. Watson-Watt originates radar.
The Arts
Literature: Steinbeck, *Tortilla Flat*; Eliot, *Murder in the Cathedral*.
Music: Gershwin, *Porgy and Bess*.
Cinema: Garbo, *Anna Karenina*; Laughton, *Mutiny on the Bounty*.

△ **October 1936:** Jarrow hunger-marchers on their way to London.

1936

January: Accession of King Edward VIII.
February: Popular Front wins Spanish elections.
March: Germany reoccupies Rhineland unopposed.
May: Italians take Addis Ababa. Mussolini proclaims annexation of Ethiopia.
June: Blum's Popular Front government in France.
July: Outbreak of Spanish Civil War. German-Austrian friendship pact.
August: Anglo-Egyptian treaty, Britain to withdraw troops except in Suez Canal Zone.
October: Berlin-Rome Axis Pact between Germany and Italy.
November: Madrid besieged. Germany and Italy recognize Franco's government. German-Japanese and Italian-Japanese Anti-Comintern agreement against the Third International. Roosevelt elected President for a second term.
December: Abdication of Edward VIII. Chiang Kai-shek kidnapped by Communists, promises to declare war on Japan.
General
Foreign powers intervene in Spain. Britain begins to rearm. Spitfire aircraft designed. S.S. *Queen Mary's* maiden voyage. Television programmes start in London. Olympic Games in Berlin.
The Arts
Literature: Mitchell, *Gone With the Wind*; Dylan Thomas, *Poems*.
Cinema: *Broadway Melody*.

1937

January: Army purges in Russia. Anglo-Italian agreement to reduce tension in Mediterranean.
March: Spanish Loyalists defeated at Brihuega. Italian-Yugoslav treaty.
May: Neville Chamberlain becomes British Prime Minister.
June: Purge of Soviet Army generals.
July: Japan resumes attacks on China.
August: Japanese capture Shanghai.
October: Germany guarantees Belgium's integrity. Franco conquers N.W. Spain. Republican government moves to Barcelona.
November: Cagoulard Fascist plot fails in France. Vargas assumes dictatorial power in Brazil.
December: Paray incident: Japanese bomb American and British ships, capture Nanking. Italy withdraws from League of Nations.
General
Chinese put up strong resistance to Japanese who behave arrogantly towards Western powers. Chamberlain adopts appeasement policy. First jet-engine. S.S. *Normandie* crosses Atlantic in 3 days 23 hours. Eyston breaks land speed record at 311 m.p.h.
The Arts
Literature: Steinbeck, *Of Mice and Men*.
Music: Britten.
Cinema: Disney, *Snow White and the Seven Dwarfs*.
Painters: Klee, Picasso, *Guernica*.

△ **1937:** Spanish peasant woman grieves for one of the half-million victims of the Civil War.

1938

February: Franco's troops capture Teruel, drive east. Hitler takes supreme command of German forces.
March: The *Anschluss*: Hitler annexes Austria. Execution of veteran Bolsheviks in Russia. Mexico seizes British and American oil companies.
April: Anglo-Irish agreement establishes friendly relations. Daladier succeeds Blum as French premier. Anglo-Italian pact.
May: Japanese make wide advances into China. Hitler visits Mussolini in Rome. German-Czech crisis over Sudetenland.
July: Russo-Japanese border fighting in E. Siberia.
September: The Munich Agreement. Czechoslovakia betrayed.
October: Japanese capture Canton and Hankow. End of Popular Front in France.
November: Russia and Poland renew non-aggression pact.
December: Franco's army drives into Catalonia.
General
Hitler's Czechoslovakian coup breaks the French alliance system in Eastern Europe. Anglo-American trade treaty marks retreat from protectionism. Introduction of nylon, ball-point pens, radar on warships, fluorescent lighting and civilian gas-masks.
The Arts
Literature: Greene, *Brighton Rock*.
Music: Bartok, R. Strauss.
Cinema: Chaplin, *Modern Times*.

1939

January: Franco captures Barcelona.
February: Britain and France recognize Franco's government.
March: Surrender of Madrid. End of Spanish Civil War. Germans occupy Czechoslovakia. Hitler annexes Memel, makes demands against Poland for Danzig.
April: Roosevelt appeals for peaceful negotiation.
May: Anglo-Turkish treaty of alliance.
August: Danzig crisis. German-Russian non-aggression pact. Britain and Poland sign pact of mutual assistance. Poles mobilize their army.
September 1st: German attack on Poland.
3rd: Britain and France declare war. Russian troops invade Poland. Rapid collapse of Polish resistance.
October: Russia makes pact with Latvia and Lithuania. Finland rejects Russian demands.
November: Russia attacks Finland.
December: Russia expelled from League of Nations.
General
While war approaches in Europe, fighting continues in China, where Russia, U.S. and Britain send supplies and loans to Chiang Kai-shek. French and British armies take up defensive positions in northern France. First serviceable helicopter in U.S., jet aircraft in Germany. Nuclear fission discovered in uranium; conscription in Britain; radar stations in operation.
The Arts
Literature: Steinbeck, *The Grapes of Wrath*.

△ **October 1938:** Germans march into the Sudetenland after Munich.

51

Who Was Who in the Thirties

△ Dollfuss, Austrian Chancellor

Benes, Eduard (1884-1948). A professor at Prague University, Benes worked for Czechoslovakian nationalism and in 1919 became foreign minister of the new state. He succeeded Masaryk as President in 1935. Relying on Franco-British support, he resisted Hitler's demands over the Sudetenland and went into exile after the betrayal of Munich. During the war, he headed the Czech government in London and returned home in 1945 to be re-elected President. After the Communist coup of 1948, he resigned his office.

Blum, Leon (1872-1950). A Parisian lawyer and writer, he became France's first Socialist Prime Minister in 1936. He headed a Popular Front government and brought in a forty-hour week, higher wages and holidays with pay. Economic difficulties and disunity of the Left-wing groups caused him to resign in 1937, though he was briefly Prime Minister again in the following year. After the Fall of France, Blum was imprisoned by the Germans until released by the Allies in 1945.

Chamberlain, Neville (1869-1940). When he succeeded Baldwin as Prime Minister of Britain in 1937, Chamberlain could count on almost universal support for his policy of appeasement towards Germany and Italy. He was a realist; he knew Britain was unready for war and her people in no mood to fight; France was weak, Russia unreliable, the League of Nations useless and the U.S. determined to stay neutral.

But his sense of realism did not extend to the dictators. By making concessions, by agreeing to Czechoslovakia's dismemberment, he merely convinced Hitler that Britain was of no account.

When he finally realized, in March 1939, that he had been duped, he applied himself to the task of rearmament. The country's indignation at the feeble performance of its armed forces in Norway caused him to yield the premiership to Churchill in 1940.

Chiang Kai-Shek (1887-1973). From 1930 to 1934, Chiang concentrated upon destroying the Communists rather than upon fighting the Japanese. However, in 1936, he agreed to a united front with Mao Tse-tung against the invader and, as generalissimo of the Chinese armies, he continued the resistance throughout World War Two.

Churchill, Winston (1871-1965). From 1929 to 1939, Churchill was out of office in the British government, because of his opposition to the National Government's India policy and, later, to appeasement. His repeated warnings against Germany's rearmament made him widely unpopular as a "warmonger". It was not until 1939 that the public changed its attitude and insisted on Chamberlain bringing him into the government as First Lord of the Admiralty.

Daladier, Edouard (1884-1970). The French Radical-Socialist leader was briefly Prime Minister in 1933 and 1934, and War Minister in the Popular Front government from 1936. Aware of France's military weakness, he supported appeasement and was one of the four who signed the Munich Agreement. During the war, he was interned by the Germans.

Dollfuss, Engelbert (1892-1934). An Austrian politician, he became Chancellor in 1932, when his country was in dire economic and political trouble. Though he opposed the Nazis, his supporters adopted their methods. After he had smashed a Socialist uprising in 1933, Dollfuss adopted dictatorial powers. The Nazis murdered him in 1934.

Edward VIII of England (1884-1972). The eldest son of King George V, he was a popular figure. As Prince of Wales, he made a number of tours and was well-liked for his informal personality and sympathy for the unemployed. He came to the throne in January 1936, but abdicated in the following December. Objections were raised to his proposed marriage to Mrs Wallis Simpson, an American whose two previous marriages had ended in divorce. He left England and, as Duke of Windsor, lived abroad for the rest of his life.

△ Franco, Spanish dictator

Franco, Francisco (1892-1975). A regular officer who had risen to command the Spanish army, Franco organized a military revolt in Morocco in 1936 and transferred his troops to Spain to fight the government. In three years of bitter warfare, he defeated the Republicans. Thereafter he ruled his country far longer than any other modern dictator. Though he was strongly pro-German, he declared Spain's neutrality in 1939 and kept her out of World War Two.

Gandhi, Mohandas K. (1869-1948). He remained India's national leader during the thirties, a saintly figure whose hold on the people's affection was actually increased when he went into religious retreat for four years. He had earlier organized civil disobedience, had been imprisoned and then released to attend the 1931 Round Table Conference in London. He emerged from retreat in 1937 to mediate between Congress and the government. When war came, he felt that only a free India could give Britain moral support. Hence, he continued to urge complete independence.

Haile Selassie (1891-1976). His coronation as Emperor of Ethiopia in 1930 marked the triumph of the Christian Church party over the Muslims and pagans. Haile Selassie had begun a programme of reform to modernize the country when the Italians launched their invasion. He remained in exile in London until 1941 when he re-entered Ethiopia with British troops to recover his throne.

△ Jean Harlow, film star

Harlow, Jean (1911-1937). The American actress who, in some ways, became a symbol of the thirties. Known as the Platinum Blonde, she played the lead in a number of films, the most famous being *Hell's Angels*. She died under mysterious circumstances at the height of her fame.

Hitler, Adolf (1889-1945). In the early thirties, Hitler emerged as a "strong man" who would solve Germany's troubles created by the Depression. He had political followers, a force of thugs to do his bidding and an orator's power to make himself heard. By 1932, he had risen high enough to stand unsuccessfully for President and, in 1933, Hindenburg accepted him as Chancellor. The agitator could surely be brought to heel inside the Cabinet.

But Hitler immediately demanded the power to pass laws without reference to the Reichstag; he crushed all opposition and swiftly turned Germany into a one-party state. This done, he could embark upon his dream of restoring Germany's greatness.

Rearmament came first—secretly, for a time, and then openly. He introduced conscription and announced the formation of a German Army. In 1936, his troops marched into the Rhineland and he used the Spanish Civil War to test his new strength.

Next, he turned to expanding Germany's frontiers. Austria was annexed in 1937; then Czechoslovakia was accused of persecuting the Sudetenland Germans. His judgement that no one was prepared to fight brought him the triumph of Munich. Six months later, he seized the rest of Czechoslovakia. Poland came under pressure with his demands for Danzig and, when Britain and France intervened with a guarantee to Poland, he replied with a master-stroke. His pact with Stalin left the way clear for the *Blitzkrieg* of September 1939.

△ Joe Louis, boxer, with his wife

Louis, Joe (1914-1981). The "Brown Bomber" is regarded by many as the greatest-ever heavyweight boxing champion. In 1935, Louis won sensational victories over Primo Carnera, the giant Italian, and Max Baer, but, in the following year, was beaten by Max Schmeling, the German champion. Louis won the world championship by beating Braddock in 1937 and, in a return bout, he knocked out Schmeling in one round. He retired undefeated in 1948.

Mao Tse-Tung (1893-1976) came from farming people in Hunan, and worked as a librarian in Peking. He studied the works of Karl Marx and joined the Chinese Communist Party when it was founded in 1921. Mao returned to his home province and became convinced that, in China, the peasants and not the urban workers would play the most important role in a future Communist revolution.

When Chiang Kai-shek launched his first attack on the Communists, Mao organized a peasants' uprising in Hunan. He had to withdraw the remains of his forces to Kiangsi, where he was joined by Chu Teh. Together, they continued to resist until Chiang's fifth extermination campaign of 1934 compelled them to undertake the Long March to Shensi.

In 1936, Mao helped to bring about the reconciliation with Chiang that enabled the Communists and the Kuomintang to combine forces against the Japanese.

△ The Marx Brothers, from left to right, Harpo, Chico and Groucho

Marx Brothers. A team of American actors, originally four in number, Groucho, Chico, Harpo and Zeppo, who made a series of brilliant film comedies which have come to be regarded as classics. They include *Animal Crackers* and *Monkey Business* (1932), *Horse Feathers* and *Duck Soup* (1933); Zeppo retired and the others made *A Night at the Opera* (1936), *A Day at the Races* (1937) and several more films in the forties.

Mussolini, Benito (1883-1945); during the thirties, Mussolini added Ethiopia and Albania to the Italian Empire. He built a powerful navy, sent aid to Franco and was one of the four signatories of the Munich Agreement.

Having raised Italy to the status of a great Power, he aimed to play as great a role in Europe as his friend Hitler. But, in fact, he had overstrained Italy's resources. While Hitler went from strength to strength, Mussolini became the junior partner who had to agree to the annexation of Austria and to tell Hitler in 1939 that he was not ready for war. Hence he made no move in September and only entered the war when the fall of France suggested the chance of some easy pickings.

△ Trotsky, exiled revolutionary

Roosevelt, Franklin, D. (1882-1945). A lawyer who entered politics as a Democrat, he was elected Governor of New York State in 1928. In the midst of the Depression in 1932, Roosevelt was nominated to stand against Hoover. His pledge of "a new deal for the American people" caught the people's imagination. He was elected President by a huge majority.

Under the New Deal, unemployment fell, business confidence recovered and when Roosevelt stood for a second term of office in 1936, the New Deal brought him another overwhelming victory.

In foreign affairs, Roosevelt adopted a "good neighbour" policy towards Latin America and Canada, while trying to urge peace upon an unresponsive Hitler.

Stalin, Josef (1879-1953). Born in Georgia and educated at a religious college, Stalin joined the Bolshevik underground movement as a young man and served under Lenin.

After the 1917 Revolution, he became a commissar in the Soviet government and general secretary of the Party. Lenin died in 1924 and Stalin was able to consolidate his grip on the Party and to isolate his rival Trotsky.

By 1929, Stalin had defeated his opponents and was able to launch his Five Year Plan to transform Russia into a powerful industrial state. Nothing was allowed to stand in his way.

During the Spanish Civil War, Stalin sent help to the Republicans without committing himself deeply and, after Munich, he signed a non-aggression pact with Hitler.

Steinbeck, John (1902-1968). An American novelist who was one of the outstanding writers of the thirties. In *Tortilla Flat* (1935), he depicted life among the poor farm-workers of California, foreshadowing his major novel *The Grapes of Wrath* (1939), a powerful account of a refugee family from the American dust bowl.

Trotsky, Lev (1879-1940). A Russian Communist leader hounded into exile by Stalin, Trotsky continued his opposition to Stalin throughout the thirties. Stalin regarded him as a dangerous threat and had him murdered in his Mexican home, in 1940.

The Press and Radio

The thirties saw the growth of mass propaganda in the dictatorships and press sensationalism in the democracies.

△ **Smudgy photograph of an object or creature believed by many to be the Loch Ness monster.** In 1933, the monster was big news; residents and visitors claimed to have seen a serpent-like creature swimming in the Scottish loch. Others declared it was a legged reptile, a kind of whale, a walrus or a giant shark. Someone said he saw it crossing a road with a sheep in its mouth.

Hydrophones were used to detect its presence; a film was made and foreign newspapers took up the story. It must have been a shy monster, for no convincing evidence was ever produced of its existence. Interest gradually waned, though it has never entirely died out.

In Russia, Germany and Italy, the press was strictly controlled by the dictators. It was the era of mass propaganda. Russian papers devoted enormous energy to promoting the official drive for rapid industrialization. Particular attention was given to stories about especially enthusiastic workers.

Goebbels was master of propaganda in Germany. A brilliant broadcaster, he used radio for mass propaganda on an unprecedented scale. The papers supported the régime with adulatory articles about the "rebirth" of Germany. Many, like the notorious *Der Sturmer* run by Julius Streicher, endorsed the official campaign against the Jews.

In Italy, despite lavish expenditure on propaganda exercises, the press was never as successfully controlled as in Russia and Germany. The anti-Fascist philosopher, Benedetto Croce, for example, was too famous for the government to touch, and continued to preach liberalism in his paper *La Critica*.

Elsewhere, the press continued in the pattern established during the twenties. The British press became brighter, snappier, in imitation of the American newspapers created by Hearst, with big headlines, staccato news items, and pages of pictures. The drive for mass circulation led to a press war in Britain, with the popular press offering all kinds of inducements, from sets of encyclopaedias to flannel trousers, in attempts to win readers away from their rivals.

The papers were full of fads and crazes designed to catch the imagination of the public. One such was the yo-yo craze of 1932, another the Loch Ness Monster story. America offered plenty of real life dramas. The careers of gangsters like John Dillinger and "Pretty Boy" Floyd, and the kidnapping of Lindbergh's baby, were followed with avid interest by a reading public hungry for sensation.

It was the age of "columnists", journalists known to the public, with regular columns. Writers like Evelyn Waugh in Britain, and Damon Runyon in America made large sums from their newspaper articles.

The press regarded radio with some suspicion but was unable to halt the growing popularity of its news bulletins, variety shows, dance band programmes and serious drama and music. Radio extended its scope—President Roosevelt introduced fireside chats to the nation, Edward VIII announced his abdication over the radio, and it was over the radio that, on 3 September 1939, Neville Chamberlain announced that Britain was at war with Germany.

◁ **A brilliant example of press photography:** the German airship *Hindenburg* bursting into flames at her mooring at Lakehurst, New Jersey on May 7, 1936. Press photographers now played an important role in journalism, for most papers carried at least one page of pictures.

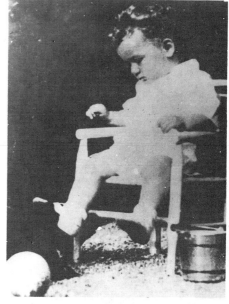

△ **Press photographers** surround Colonel Lindbergh during the time of the kidnapping.

△ **Kidnapped child,** Charles Lindbergh Jnr.

Lindbergh's Baby

In 1932, the whole world was moved by the kidnapping of the Lindbergh baby, one of the biggest press stories of the thirties. For his solo crossing of the Atlantic in 1927 and his subsequent feats as a flier, Charles Lindbergh had become America's Number One hero. Publicity brought tragedy to his family when, in March 1932, their baby son was kidnapped from his bedroom.

A $50,000 dollar ransom was handed over to a man with a foreign accent but, while the world waited for news, the child was not returned. He was found dead a few days later. Then followed the laborious tracing of every ransom note until, in 1934, police arrested Richard Hauptmann, a German immigrant. He was tried and found guilty; after lengthy appeals, Hauptmann went to the electric chair. By this time, the Lindberghs had gone to England to escape publicity.

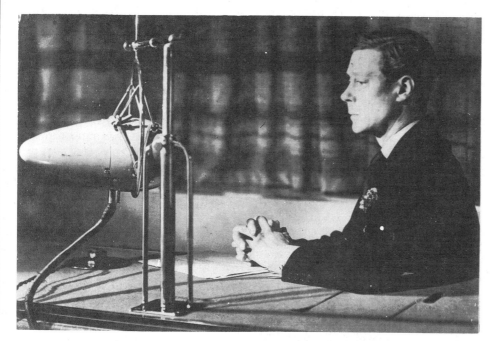

△ **King Edward VIII** broadcasts to the nation. He abdicated in Dec. 1936.

△ **The Duke and Duchess of Windsor in** June 1937, on their wedding day.

Abdication of Edward VIII

The biggest story of 1936 was Britain's Abdication crisis, a story too big for its press to handle at first. For months, foreign papers had carried stories of King Edward's friendship with Mrs Wallis Simpson, but the general public knew nothing.

In November, a bishop chose to rebuke the King and the Press came out with the story. The King wished to marry a twice-divorced American; Prime Minister Stanley Baldwin, the Cabinet, Dominions' governments and most influential people were against the match. The people were for the King but, on December 10, Edward abdicated and left the country. He took the title of Duke of Windsor and married Mrs Simpson in France in 1937.

Science

Many of the scientific discoveries made in the thirties were later used in military devices in World War Two.

The most dramatic work occurred in the field of atomic research (see below). Radio astronomy had its beginning in Reber's dish-type radio telescope and radar, which was to help to win the Battle of Britain, owed its development to Watson-Watt, the British scientist, and to Breit and True in America.

New materials, such as aluminium, polythene (1933), nylon (1939) and synthetic rubber were produced, as well as a nickel chrome alloy for use in jet engines. Frank Whittle was working on jet propulsion as early as 1930; a successful jet engine was built in 1937 and two years later the first jet plane, a Heinkel, flew in Germany.

Scientists also applied themselves to the problems of agriculture to increase yields and improve the quality of crops and livestock. Research establishments, notably the one at Rothamsted in England, were set up to study soils, plants, animals, fruits and farming economy.

Through scientific crossbreeding, grain crops and grasses were greatly improved, while the chemists produced new fertilizers to increase yields. Silos and artificial driers came into use, together with weed-control and crop-spraying against pests. Many farmers were still using draught animals, mainly horses, but tractors were becoming more common, along with improved threshing-machines, reapers, binders and corn-harvesters.

In medical science, the discovery and isolation of vitamins made news; immunization against yellow-fever was introduced, W. R. Park produced a vaccine for polio, and sulphanilomide drugs (M & B) made their appearance.

Among the innumerable practical discoveries of the thirties we can mention the ballpoint pen, an amphibious tank, the first parking meter, pedestrian crossings and automatic traffic signals. DDT made its appearance and so did sound-proofing, an electrostatic copying process, and the absolute altimeter to prevent air crashes over mountains. The theory of electronic computers was already understood.

△ **Milk churns made of aluminium,** a metal which came into everyday use in the thirties, thanks to electrolysis—chemical decomposition by electrical action.

◁ **Early "accelerator",** devised by J. D. Cockroft and E. T. S. Walton, the British atomic scientists who observed disintegration of a nucleus under impact of artificially accelerated particles. Following upon Rutherford's discovery that the nucleus of the atom could be split, scientists such as Cockroft and Walton, Compton, Urey and Millikan in the U.S., Joliot in France, Hahn and Strassman in Germany worked out a new kind of physics. They explored properties of matter, the inner structure of the atom and its nucleus. Their work led to the nuclear explosions which ended World War Two and also to more positive uses of atomic energy.

The Record Breakers

Increased speed on land, water and in the air became possible through technical advances, so the public was thrilled by a succession of records by popular heroes.

Malcolm Campbell was knighted for his record-breaking runs in *Bluebird*, the Englishman, Kay Don, and the American Gar

Wood, regularly broke each other's motor-boat speed records. Pilots like Jim and Amy Mollison, Jean Batten and Amelia Earhart made record flights about the world to establish permanent air routes. The first flight over Mount Everest was made in April, 1933.

In these last years of steam, Britain's railway companies vied with each other and with American and German locomotives to set up new speeds over both long and short distances. The record for a steam locomotive, established by the *Mallard* in 1938, remained unbroken until 1973.

△ **Sir Malcolm Campbell** with *Bluebird* in which he broke the world land speed record in 1931, 1933 and 1937 (301 m.p.h.).

△ **Campbell turned to boats** and in *Bluebird* (above) broke the world's speed-boat record in 1938 and 1939 (144.74 m.p.h.).

△ **The Class A4 locomotive** *Mallard* which, pulling a load of seven coaches, broke the world's speed record for steam traction in 1938. In beating its rivals *Coronation* and *Silver Fox*, it reached 126 m.p.h.

△ **The Cunard White Star liner** *Queen Mary* broke the Atlantic crossing record in 1936, lost it to the *Normandie* in 1937 and regained it with an average speed of 31.69 knots (3 days, 20 hours, 42 minutes).

Land Speed Records

1931	Campbell (Napier-Campbell)	246.09 m.p.h.	Britain
1932	Campbell (Napier-Campbell)	253.97 m.p.h.	Britain
1933	Campbell (Rolls-Royce-Campbell)	272.46 m.p.h.	Britain
1935	Campbell (Bluebird Special)	276.82 m.p.h.	Britain
1935	Campbell (Bluebird Special)	301.13 m.p.h.	Britain
1937	Eyston (Thunderbolt)	312.00 m.p.h.	Britain
1938	Eyston (Thunderbolt)	345.50 m.p.h.	Britain
1938	Cobb (Railton)	350.20 m.p.h.	Britain
1938	Eyston (Thunderbolt)	357.50 m.p.h.	Britain
1939	Cobb (Railton)	369.70 m.p.h.	Britain

Air Speed Records

1931	Stainforth (Supermarine S.6B)	388.00 m.p.h.	Britain
1931	Stainforth (Supermarine S.6B)	407.02 m.p.h.	Britain
1931	Stainforth (Supermarine S.6B)	415.20 m.p.h.	Britain
1934	Agello (Macchi-Castoldi 72)	423.85 m.p.h.	Italy
1934	Agello (Macchi-Castoldi 72)	430.32 m.p.h.	Italy
1934	Bernascori (Macchi-Castoldi 72)	434.96 m.p.h.	Italy
1934	Agello (Macchi-Castoldi 72)	440.69 m.p.h.	Italy
1934	Agello (Macchi-Castoldi 72)	441.22 m.p.h.	Italy
1939	Dieterle (Heinkel He 100V-8)	463.92 m.p.h.	Germany
1939	Wendel (Messerschmitt Bf 109R)	469.22 m.p.h.	Germany
1939	Wendel (Messerschmitt Bf 109R)	486.00 m.p.h.	Germany

Electric Motors

Electricity was used on an increasingly large scale during the thirties. These projects show how to use simple electric motors.

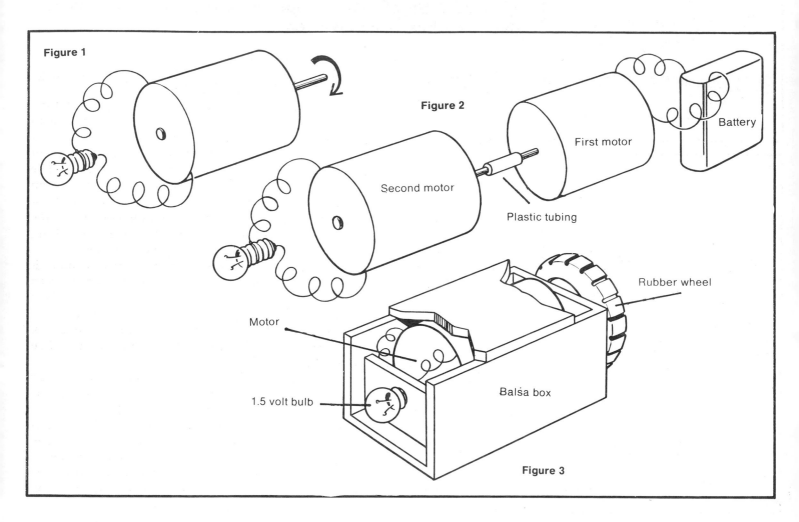

Figure 1

Figure 2

First motor

Battery

Second motor

Plastic tubing

Rubber wheel

Motor

1.5 volt bulb

Balsa box

Figure 3

Generators
A simple electric motor can work as a dynamo or *generator* of electricity when it is made to rotate. Motors of this sort are very inexpensive, and can be obtained from most model or electrical shops. The motor will probably have two wires connected to it. If not, attach two short lengths of insulated wire to the terminals on the motor.

Figure 1 shows how a motor can be used to run a torch bulb. Connect the terminal wires to the bulb, as shown in the diagram. Grasp the spindle of the motor between thumb and forefinger, and use a flicking motion to spin the motor over rapidly. The bulb should light and then fade as the motor slows down.

Figure 2 shows the principle on which big electricity generators work. Join two motors with a piece of plastic tubing, and connect a battery to the first motor.

The battery is the power source, the first motor is the *turbine*, and the second motor is the *generator*.

This set-up is not very efficient as an electric power source (the battery) is used to produce electricity. The power source of a full-scale generator is usually steam, gas, or water.

Electric brake
The set-ups in Figure 1 and Figure 2 can both be used to demonstrate how an electric brake works. Instead of connecting the terminal wires to the bulb, short the two ends by connecting them.

The *generator* will now be very stiff to turn over, either by hand or by the battery. Shorting the output leads has turned an electric motor into an electric brake—a system used on electrically powered vehicles like trams and trolley buses.

Figure 3 shows how to make a batteryless torch. Connect a small motor to a bulb and mount them in a small box built out of sheet balsa. Leave the motor spindle sticking out of one end. Fit a rubber tyred wheel to the end of the spindle, gluing it in place with a strong adhesive. Spinning this wheel rapidly will light the torch. The heavier the wheel the better, as it will act as a flywheel, keeping the motor spinning longer.

Diagram A

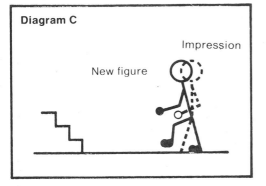

Diagram B

Impression from first page

Diagram C

Impression

New figure

Diagram D

Impression from second page

New figure

Flicker Books

Animated cartoon films became enormously popular during the thirties. "Flicker books" work on the same principle as cartoons. A simple image, repeated with gradual variations, gives the illusion of movement.

Scribble pads about 5 in. x 4 in., or any notebook with plain pages of about the same size, can be used to make flicker books. Draw your own animated cartoon stories, a page at a time.

The subject to be described is a man approaching some steps, but the same principles apply to any cartoon sequence.

Use a fairly hard pencil (H or HB) and draw a horizontal line to represent the ground, and lines to represent the steps. At one side draw a figure standing upright, pressing hard on the pencil (**diagram A**).

On the second page you should see an impression of the drawing on the first page. Draw in the ground and steps in exactly the same positions (**diagram B**). Then draw in the figure again, but this time start to show movement by drawing one leg raised, and the body tilted forward (**diagram C**).

Now turn to the third page, again copying the ground and steps exactly, but showing the figure in a further stage of movement (**diagram D**). Continue in this way, making the figure walk up the steps and disappear off the left-hand

side of the page. If the drawing goes wrong at any stage, cut out that page and start again.

Whatever the sequence, the method is the same. You need a static background, like a ground line, which is repeated page after page, and movement on the part of the main subject. The impression made by the drawing on one page serves as a guide for positioning the drawing on the next. Once the sequence is complete, you can ink in, or even paint in, the drawings.

The important thing to remember is that to produce smooth movement, seen when you flick through the pages of the book, the changes in position must be very gradual. A sudden change of position will show up as a jerk when viewed.

The thicker the book the longer the cartoon story you can make—but the more individual drawings you will have to tackle. Start with fairly short stories —say about 30 to 40 pages—until you have mastered the basic technique. Then you can attempt a really long sequence, joining two or more books together, if necessary.

▽ **Figures are quite easy to draw, but as a guide three typical movements are given below:** walking, running and jumping.

Remember that when you come to draw the figures in the flicker book, the changes from one body position to another must be made

very gradually.

If you do have trouble drawing figures, then you can tackle stories where the subject moves as a whole in simple steps, rather than having forward movement combined with movement of arms and legs. You can

show the sun rising above the horizon, a tree growing, or a flower opening its petals, for example. You can show a car, ship or plane moving from right to left across the page— and show another coming in the opposite direction, so that they pass, or meet head-on!

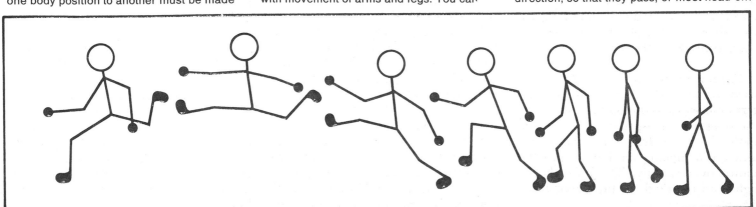

Cartoons

The fads and fashions of the decade provided targets for cartoonists whose style was still ponderously Victorian.

In these cartoons from *Punch*, we see some of the topics which diverted the British middle-classes during the thirties. Unemployment and international tension have no place in this world where the latest fashions and innovations are treated with a benevolent humour which is funny by being so feeble. However, *Punch* was not the journal for acid social comment.

The drawings require lengthy explanation. Modern cartoons are much slicker; indeed, they often dispense altogether with words.

△ **Hostess: "Will you take this chair, Uncle?"**
Uncle: "As long as I don't have to sit on it, my dear." The latest styles in "modernistic" decor are regarded with amused disdain by the older generation.

▷ **Owner: "Do tell me you loathe it."** The thirties saw the appearance of numbers of "ultra-modern" houses. Avant-garde owners had to contend with ridicule and anger.

△ **"Sorry, Daddy, but we had to do something about it. The giddy flapper is out of date."** Rejecting backless gowns, the girls adopt styles which are comically old-fashioned.

▷ **"Am I to take it from this window that the latest fashion is to be no bathing-costumes at all?"** The sun-bathing craze was a boon to cartoonists of the period.

△ **"I don't think we've quite got the hang of the instrument yet, Miss Smith."** Innovations like dictaphones were looked upon as ridiculous new-fangled contraptions.

△ **Castles in the Air.** Motor-bikes were popular with many who could not afford a car—to the annoyance of those who could (see below).

▽ **Man with particular grievance: "Oh, it's only you, is it? I thought it was one of those confounded motor cycles kicking up a row."**

△ **Provincial Person: "Can _anyone_ go in here?"** In the film industry's hey-day, super cinemas provided dream-like luxury.

△ **"You see what they're doing, Emily? Taking him for a ride. Presently we shall see them sock him and possibly bump him off."** Gangster films became so popular that even old ladies became familiar with American slang. Edward G. Robinson was one of the Hollywood stars who played gangster roles.

△ **"Yes, yes, this is Private Whetherstone, 2709385, speaking."** When conscription was introduced in 1938, the rich were supposed to join up in the ranks like everyone else.

△ **"I trust Madam will excuse me if I leave her for a moment? We have a slight outbreak of fire on the ground floor."** A skit on the perils of undergoing a permanent wave.

Index

Further Reading

Available in the United States and Canada:

ALLEN, FREDERICK LEWIS. *Since Yesterday;* Harper & Row, 1972. *The American Heritage History of the 20's and 30's.* American Heritage, 1970.
BURNS, JAMES MACGREGOR. *The Lion and the Fox.* Harcourt Brace Jovanovich, 1956.
FEIS, HERBERT. *The Road to Pearl Harbor: The Coming of the War Between the United States and Japan.* Princeton University Press, 1971.
FREIDEL, FRANK. *Franklin D. Roosevelt: Launching the New Deal.* Little, Brown, 1973.
GRIFFITH, RICHARD and ARTHUR MAYER. *The Movies.* Simon & Schuster, 1957.
GUNTHER, JOHN. *Roosevelt in Retrospect.* Harper & Row, 1950.
LASH, JOSEPH P. *Eleanor and Franklin Roosevelt: The Story of Their Relationship Based on Eleanor Roosevelt's Private Papers.* Norton, 1971.
LEUCHTENBURG, WILLIAM E. *Franklin D. Roosevelt and the New Deal, 1932-1940.* Harper & Row, 1963.
LEUCHTENBURG, WILLIAM E. *The Life History of the United States, Vol. II, 1933-1945: New Deal and Global War.* Time, 1964.
SCHLESINGER, ARTHUR M., JR. *Age of Roosevelt, Vol. 2, Coming of the New Deal.* Houghton Mifflin, 1959.
SHANNON, DAVID A., ed. *The Great Depression.* Prentice-Hall, 1960.
SHERWOOD, ROBERT E. *Roosevelt and Hopkins: An Intimate History.* Harper & Row, 1950.
SIMON, RITA JAMES, ed. *As We Saw the Thirties; Essays on Social and Political Move-ments of a Decade.* University of Illinois Press, 1967.
SLOAN, ALFRED P., JR. *My Years with General Motors.* Doubleday, 1964. *This Fabulous Century, Vol. 4, 1930-1940.* Time, 1969.
TOLAND, JOHN. *The Dillinger Days.* Random House, 1963.
WHITEHEAD, DONALD. *The F.B.I. Story.* Random House, 1956.
WILSON, EDMUND. *American Earthquake: A Documentary of the Jazz Age, the Great Depression, and the New Deal.* Octagon Books, 1971.

Available in Britain:

BLYTHE, R. *Age of Illusion:* Britain in the Twenties and Thirties. Hamilton 1963; Penguin 1964.
BRANSON, N. *Britain in the Nineteen Thirties.* Weidenfeld & Nicolson 1971.
BRYANT, A. *The Lion and the Unicorn.* Collins 1969.
GILBERT, B. *Britain Since 1918.* Batsford 1967.
GRAVES, R. & HODGE, A. *The Long Weekend:* a social history of Great Britain 1918-1939. Methuen 1955; Penguin 1971.
HEMINGWAY, E. *For Whom the Bell Tolls.* (1940) Penguin 1955.
ISHERWOOD, C. *Goodbye to Berlin.* (1939) Penguin 1945.
LAVER, J. *Between the Wars.* Vista 1961.
MALRAUX, A. *Days of Hope.* (1938) Penguin 1970.
McELWEE, W. *Britain's Locust Years 1918-1940.* Faber 1962.
MOWAT, C. *Britain Between the Wars 1918-1940.* Methuen 1955.
MUGGERIDGE, M. *The Thirties.* Collins 1967; Fontana 1971.
ORWELL, G. *The Road to Wigan Pier.* (1937) Penguin 1962.
ORWELL, G. *Homage to Catalonia.* (1938) Penguin 1962.
SNOW, E. *Red Star Over China.* Pelican 1972.
STANDEN, J. *After the Deluge:* English society between the wars. Faber 1969.
STEINBECK, J. *Grapes of Wrath.* (1939) Penguin 1951.
SYMONS, J. *The Thirties.* Cresset 1960.
SYMONS, J. *Between the Wars:* Britain in Photographs. Batsford 1972.
TEED, P. *Britain 1908-1960:* a welfare state. Hutchinson 1967.

Acknowledgements

Special Adviser

Dr J. M. Roberts, Fellow and Tutor in Modern History at Merton College, Oxford

Editor

Sue Jacquemier

Assistant Editor

Tim Healey

Projects Author

R. H. Warring *p. 58-9*

Cover picture: Spectators watching a competitor in the Schneider Trophy race for seaplanes, held throughout the thirties.

Back cover: Distressed family and unemployed workers; from a British election poster of 1931.

Note: in this book all foreign words, titles of books, films, plays, etc., are *in italics*, e.g. *Grapes of Wrath*.

If we have unwittingly infringed copyright in any picture or photograph reproduced in this publication, we tender our sincere apologies and will be glad of the opportunity, upon being satisfied as to the owner's title, to pay an appropriate fee as if we had been able to obtain prior permission.

We wish to thank the following individuals and organizations for their assistance and for making available material in their collections.

Key to picture positions:

(T) top (C) centre (L) left (B) bottom (R) right and combinations; for example: (TC) top centre.

Aluminium Federation *p. 56(TL)*
Archiv Gerstenberg *p. 12(R)*
Art Institute of Chicago *p. 19(BR)*
Associated Press *p. 17(TR), 53(R)*
AZ-Archiv, Vienna *p. 50(B)*
Bibliothèque Nationale *p. 10(T), 39(BL), 40(T)*
BOAC *p. 24 (C), 24-5*
British Rail *p. 8(BR)*
Bundesarchiv, Koblenz *p. 2, 13(T), 31(B), 14(T), 14(BR), 15(BL), 16(BL)*
Cavendish Laboratory, University of Cambridge *p. 56(B)*
Chin Antiques *p. 10(BL)*
Condé Nast *p. 8(BL)*
Conservative Research Dept. *back cover, p. 7(B)*
County Borough of Blackpool *p. 35(T)*
David Drummond Collection *p. 24(L)*
Editions Rencontre *p. 37, 47(TR)*
Esquire Magazine *p. 18(R)*
George Allen & Unwin *p. 27(CL)*
George Orwell Archive *p. 42(L)*
Granada Theatres Ltd. *p. 11(T)*
Harlingue-Viollet *p. 6(B)*
Historical Research Unit *p. 13(CR), 38(L)*
Huntingdon-Hartford *p. 1*
Hulton Picture Library *p. 6(T), 7(TL), 8(TL), 25(T), 45(TC), 51(T), 52(C), 52(R), 55(BL), 57(TL), 57(TR), 57(BR)*
Institute of Social History, Amsterdam *p. 27(CC)*
International Press Agency *p. 5(B)*
Keystone Press *p. 51(B), 53(L), 54(T), 54(B), 55(TL),*
55(TR), 55(BR)
King Features Syndicate *p. 20(BL)*
Kladderadtsch *p. 30(T)*
Leni Riefenstahl *p. 42(R)*
Library of Congress *p. 7(TR), 21(T), 21(BL), 21(BR), 30(B), 31(B)*
L'Illustration p. 35(BL)
Macdonald Visual Books *p. 17(BR), 25(B), 28(TR), 28(BR)*
Mansell *p. 9(T), 9(BL), 9(BR)*
National Archives, Washington *p. 19(BL), 20(BR), 51(C)*
Nebelspalter *p. 46(TL)*
Novosti *p. 27(CR)*
Pennsylvania Academy of Fine Arts *p. 18(L)*
Popper, Paul *p. 16(TL), 44(R), 50(T)*
Punch p. 34(BL), 60-1
Robert Kingston Films Ltd. *p. 44(L)*
Roger Viollet *p. 23, 32(B), 39(CR)*
Science Museum *p. 35(BR)*
Shellmex & B.P. Ltd. *p. 28(BL)*
Snark/SPADEM *p. 14(BL)*
Stanley Gibbons Ltd. *p. 32(T), 39(TR), 39(BR)*
Südd-Verlag *p. 4(BR), 46(BL), 47(TL), 49(B)*
U.F.A. *p. 45(BR), 52(L)*
Ullstein *p. 12(L)*
Understanding p. 33(BR)
United Press International *p. 50(C)*
Walt Disney Inc. *p. 45(TR)*

Artists and photographers

Barker, Chris *p. 11(T)*
Capa, Robert *p. 40-1*
Coppola *front cover*
Hajek, Karel *p. 47(B)*
Munch, Janet/Freelance Presentations *p. 25(C), 29(TL), 29(TR), 29(CR), 29(BR)*
Ringart, Noel, Paris *p. 36(BR)*
Taylor, Peter *p. 5(T), 5(C), 29(BL), 31(T), 33(T), 38(T), 38(R), 41,*